D1738641

Pick Your Pieces

Some Thoughts To Think About

Joseph Plummer

Contents

Acknowledgements

First, I want to thank *you* for caring enough about yourself and the world to read a book like this. As of 2023, we're facing some very difficult social, personal, and political challenges. The upside is that these challenges are forcing us to find healthier ways to cope and overcome. It's counterintuitive, but the "bad" is paving the way for the better. We are making progress because of people like you.

Second, I've also got to thank my old friend Jim Principi. Jim, your sincere interest in this material, along with your encouragement and feedback, kept this project moving along. Thanks to you, I finally stopped "thinking about" writing this book and, instead, actually got it done. "Pick Your Pieces" is here in 2023 (rather than 2033) because of you!

Preface

This is not a political book, but it *is* an attempt to facilitate the creation of a competing parallel system—a system that you can build within yourself, a psychological system that protects against the onslaught of modern-day challenges and programming that we all have to endure.

Except for the introduction, most of this book consists of separate, stand-alone passages under 200 words each. (For context, the introduction covers the absolute mess I was when I was younger, and the short passages cover the ideas and perspectives that not only helped me unwind that mess but continue to help me decades later.)

I sincerely hope you'll grab a pen or pencil and, as you're reading, highlight passages that speak to you, and use the "notes" section to record why. Likewise, if you're bothered by a particular passage, write out your argument against it. Consider creating your own index of passages that you want to revisit again. Bottom line: Mark this book up; make it your own. Lastly, be patient with this material. When you encounter ideas that require more thought (an hour, a day, a week or longer), set the book down and give yourself some time. You'll gain more.

Please, if you find this information useful:

1. Let others know that they can read for free at PickYourPieces.com.
2. Leave a rating or short review at Amazon or your preferred book review site(s).
3. If you *really* like it, pick up a copy for somebody you care about.

Introduction
Quality of Life

What *really* determines our quality of life? Some believe it boils down to whether or not we have lots of money or talent or beauty or popularity. But the world is filled with people who, despite having these things, are miserable nonetheless. (Some of them are even suicidal.) How about physical health? No again. There are lots of people who possess perfect physical health, yet live in a state of constant anger, resentment, fear, or depression. Is it about having a great family and great friends? Apparently not. Some of the most unhappy and self-destructive people in the world are dearly loved, surrounded by friends and family who desperately want to help them but, sadly, cannot.

So, what is it? What ultimately determines the quality of a person's life experience? Maybe it's not a "what." Maybe it's a "who." And maybe that "who" exists as an identity that we've created and interact with in our daily lives. When we interact with pieces of our identity that are healthy, we experience a better relationship with our mind and with our

notes:_____

_____

_____

life. However, to the extent we interact with pieces that are unhealthy, we move toward habits of thought and behavior that are self-destructive and ultimately lead to suffering. In a worst-case scenario, we might falsely conclude that these self-destructive pieces are more powerful than we are. They're not. In fact, within a healthier identity of our making, they couldn't even exist.

In a nutshell, that's what this book is about. It's about the "pieces" that we pick up and unconsciously incorporate into our identity. It's about the natural process by which this happens and the dramatic effect it has on our lives. Above all, the short passages in this book aim at weakening the unhealthy pieces—pieces that undermine the process of beneficial identity creation.

Let's start with a few ideas:

1. We can acquire habitual thoughts and behaviors that cause us unnecessary harm.
2. Some of the harms are so integrated into our identity, and so prevalent in our culture, that we don't even see them.
3. Our personal challenges are infinitely unique, but our mental and/or physical response tends to fall under one of two categories: helpful or harmful.

notes:_____

_____

_____

Since the easiest way to illustrate the three ideas above is through a story, I'll tell the story I'm most familiar with: My own. Here, I'll briefly cover some of the unique experiences, challenges, and bad responses I chose as a kid, along with the realizations that prevented me from completely destroying my life.

A QUICK HISTORY:

I had an unusual upbringing that led to unusual opportunities and plenty of bad choices. I was 10 years old when I began smoking pot and drinking alcohol. By age 13, supply permitting, I was getting high daily. My goals in life were pretty simple: Hang out with my friends, get stoned, listen to music, and chase girls. I considered myself a "stoner," and I pursued that lifestyle 24/7. Not surprisingly, this led to many undesirable outcomes. I was physically, emotionally, and spiritually unhealthy. I was unreliable and insecure. I was a coward who'd pick on weaker kids, but I'd back down in a second from a legitimate challenge. I stole to get drug money or other things that I wanted; I vandalized property, broke into houses, cars, schools. Basically, at a remarkably young age, I'd become a complete asshole. If I had a single redeeming quality, it was my conscience. It nagged at me. It made me feel gross and disappointing. But there was a solution for that: Get high, put on some tunes, hook up with a girl, and worry about it later.

notes:_____

_____

_____

With effort, I was able to ignore my conscience for many years. Then, one night while lying in bed (age 14), something broke the final straw in my mind. Truths I'd refused to face and issues I needed to deal with had boxed me in. None of the normal justifications for my choices were working; no lies were sufficient. I hated who I was, and it hurt—bad. In that moment, a different version of myself began to appear in my mind—a version that I desperately wanted to be. (A *potential* version that, if I didn't change, would never get a chance to live.)

Standing over me in my mind's eye, I saw my opposite. A person with self-respect. A person who wasn't so small inside that they needed to bully others, and was big enough inside to fight (win or lose) when necessary. I saw a person who possessed a type of power I'd never developed: integrity. One who could be counted on and trusted. An individual that was patient and always did their best. I saw a person who truly knew the pitfalls and inherent weakness of dishonesty and had become too wise to even consider it—my opposite, indeed.

I studied that human for a couple hours and imagined how much different my life would be if I tried to be more like him. The clarity and power of the experience was non-negotiable. It *forced* me to let go of all the lies, and, to my amazement, I felt liberated. For the first time in my life, I knew what

notes:_____

_____

_____

I needed to do: Stop running, *accept responsibility for my choices*, and grow up. Then and there, I committed myself to that goal.

I'd love to say that the intense experience triggered an overnight transformation, but it didn't. I stopped smoking pot for a couple weeks, felt uncomfortable around my friends, and then ran back to my old identity and habits. I didn't revisit the goal until 1985 when, at the age of 15, I received a sentence of one to six years behind bars. Fortunately, I only had to serve nine months, but that was long enough. It provided plenty of time to reflect and finally accept *full* responsibility for my choices and their consequences. That's when my trajectory permanently changed for the better.

I was released from jail about a week prior to my 16th birthday, and over the next few years, I slowly inched my way toward developing the traits I'd visualized when I was 14. Day One, I started with quitting pot, no more stealing, and no more bullying. Then, I progressed to regular exercise, eating healthy, and learning the confidence-building benefits of being honest. By age 19, I'd made a lot of progress. I was definitely a better person—as long as I wasn't drunk.

From age 16 to 21, I was basically a weekend drinker, and as long as I didn't drink too much, everything seemed OK.

notes:_____

_____

_____

Unfortunately, when I *did* drink too much, remnants of the "old me" emerged with a vengeance. My highlight reel included things like breaking into a closed pizza shop to make myself dinner (embarrassed beyond words, I went to the police and turned myself in the next day); standing in a suburban subdivision and repeatedly loading and then unloading a 38 revolver into the ground (that fiasco made the local newspaper); kicking out arresting officers' back windows, fighting, shouting, making a monumental ass out of myself; and racking up more driving violations than most *families* do in a lifetime.

Despite the progress I'd made, my drinking threatened to destroy my life in an instant. That realization led me to "stop drinking" many times,[1] but it wasn't until March 28, 1991 (three days after receiving my fourth DUI), that I got it right and stopped for good. *Finally*, I'd conquered my inner idiot, and all would be well!...No, not exactly.

For some reason, I assumed that sobriety would end my suffering once and for all. I was wrong. Yes, it ended the suffering associated with getting drunk, doing stupid shit, and then paying the price, but sobriety brought a new challenge. I hadn't yet developed the ability to deal with unmedicated

---

[1] Once I fully accepted that alcohol was the enemy of everything I hoped to achieve, I mercilessly attacked any remaining thoughts/impulses to consume it. Fortunately, I never accepted the "disease" diagnosis I'd been given (I never accepted I was a "powerless" alcoholic), and that helped me as I rewired my habitual thoughts surrounding alcohol. Within six months of abstinence, my mind was much stronger. Within a year, abstinence was effortless. If you're interested, I've provided more details at HowToStopDrinking.org.

reality. I'd been using drugs and alcohol to avoid unpleasant thoughts and emotions for more than half my life. My brain developed from childhood through adulthood with that crutch, and now the crutch was gone. My outward behavior was where it needed to be (no cheating, no stealing, no drugs, no alcohol, etc.), but the intensity of my reactions to the outside world became nearly intolerable. I tortured myself with negative perspectives. I exaggerated the significance of things I considered "bad" and blinded myself to all that was good. In short, my inner idiot was alive and well. He still held power and was using it to create dangerous states of hopelessness and depression. This went on for six years until I *finally* realized that "he" wasn't "me."

The small piece of my identity that created depression was no different than the piece that formerly created a desire to smoke pot daily. It was no different than the piece that formerly drove my desire to drink. No different than the other pieces that justified lying, stealing, cheating, etc. Each was just a piece of identity—a circuit in my brain—that I nurtured with false beliefs and associations. I successfully eliminated and replaced the other unhealthy pieces; so why did it take me half a decade before I figured out that I could do the same with the piece creating depression? Hindsight provides the answer: I'd recognized the earlier pieces as my enemy because they inspired behaviors that undermined who I wanted to be. They created an immediate conflict, and that enabled me to choose a side. But the depression was different. It was rooted in a piece of my *accepted* identity. It was so firmly integrated into who I *thought* I was, I'd never even thought to question it, despite its clearly destructive impact on my life.[2]

That lesson was the most profound I've experienced in the 53 years I've been on this planet. It led me to discover what I firmly believe is the most important job we have: to guard against and eliminate "pieces" of identity (accepted thoughts, impulses, and behaviors) that turn our own energy against us. By doing so, we free up a tremendous amount of energy for our second most important job: to develop and strengthen pieces of identity that empower us and improve the quality of our life, regardless of our circumstances. By committing myself to those two jobs, I made more progress in the year that followed than I'd made at any other point in my life. Best of all, decades later, that progress continues.

If nothing else, I hope the short passages in this book will help you *experience* the following truth for yourself: Effortless abstinence from destructive thoughts, impulses, and behaviors and effortless fidelity to constructive thoughts, impulses, and behaviors are *both* achievable. They're the

---

[2]   I was an uncontrollable kid, and that led to plenty of psychologists, psychological tests, and interventions *prior* to my 15th birthday. I still remember the first time an "expert" diagnosed me as having ADD. I remember interpreting the diagnosis as him saying, "His bad behavior isn't his fault." I liked the sound of that. When I was later diagnosed as being "neurotic," I liked the sound of that even more. But when I was diagnosed as having a "chemical imbalance," I embraced that completely. I was now certifiably crazy! My intense mood swings had nothing to do with my life choices or how I interpreted myself and the world; nope, my problems were caused by my "manic depressive disorder." I was bipolar! Unfortunately, I picked that "piece of identity" up very young and never questioned it. I'm very grateful to have finally seen and overcome it, and I'm even more grateful that (as of 2023) there is now significant scientific pushback against the chemical-imbalance diagnosis.

inevitable result of carefully monitoring and deliberately rewiring your mind. And though the rewiring process *itself* takes some effort and patience, the rewards last a lifetime.

NOTE: The main ideas in this book are covered many times in slightly different ways. For instance, the ego, the automatic mind, mental circuits, programs, the inner idiot, and even "pieces of identity" all basically refer to the same thing. The different terms and analogies provide alternate paths to the same primary idea: that "you" are none of these things. You are the awareness that can distance itself from harmful thoughts and acquired identity, observe them both, and make changes (large and small) that transform your life for the better.

notes:_____

_____

_____

CHAPTER 1

Mental Machinery

(1)

Have you ever noticed that most of your mental and physical activity is completely automated? It's true. That amazing brain of yours is constantly creating mental circuits that reduce the need for you to *think*.

When it comes to physical activities, we understand this process as "learning how" to do something. Take riding a bike for example. If you plan on acquiring this skill, it's going to take some serious focus, thought, and effort at first. But then, like magic, the thinking stops, the wobbling stops, the falling over stops, and suddenly you've got it. From then forward, staying upright and in control is practically effortless. But how did this happen? Well, without realizing it, you helped your brain grow new physical connections that didn't exist before. Those new mental circuits are now doing what they were programmed to do so that you can focus your conscious mind on other things.

notes:_____

_____

_____

OK, that's how it works with physical activities, but what about activities that are purely mental? What about the inner voice that reacts to a news headline, a social media post, aches and pains, or the death of a loved one? What about bad mental habits; common inner narratives and impulses that inevitably lead to unnecessary suffering? Unfortunately, your brain automates these things too. And once the unhealthy circuit is established (just like riding a bike), it'll effortlessly bypass your conscious mind and take you for a ride. But there's a very important difference.

Unlike riding a bike, you never consciously choose to create many of the circuits that influence your daily thoughts, feelings, impulses, and behaviors. Instead, you picked them up *unconsciously*, when you were young, before you possessed the maturity and wisdom to assess their value. And now, those circuits continue doing what they were designed to do, regardless of whether or not it's a good idea.

It's just a fact of human biology: We're born with a brain that will automate anything, including unhealthy mental activity. But the good news is, we can teach our brain to recognize and uninstall its unhealthy circuits; we can replace them with circuits of our choosing. This is absolutely one of the greatest powers that human beings possess. Scientists call it self-directed neuroplasticity; I call it *choosing* to rewire your

notes:_____

_____

_____

mind. Whatever you want to call it, discover and strengthen your ability to do this. It'll improve your life in ways that you can hardly imagine.

(2)
Our mental programs express the personality and level of consciousness that created them.

(3)
You have one very important job in this life: Recognize that *YOU* are the programmer, not the programs. You are the one who can identify undesirable circuits in your brain and, through deliberate conscious effort, weaken and replace them.

(4)
Deliberate transformation begins with imagining ourselves as the person we *want* to be. By visualizing the desired traits of our future self, we create a map in our mind, a map that illustrates our path and the distance we've yet to travel. Suddenly, habits that impede our progress become obvious. They clash with the vision we've created, and they force the mind to choose: Abandon the vision, or continue eliminating bad habits that stand in its way. If you struggle to imagine who you want to be, start by imagining who you *don't* want to be. This too will reveal habits that need to be eliminated.

notes:_____

_____

_____

(5)

My typical stages of intentional rewiring:

Stage 1: I suddenly notice a mental and/or physical habit that I should change. (Prior to that moment, I wasn't consciously aware of the problem.)

Stage 2: I eventually commit to change and begin the process by consistently challenging the unwanted habit of thought or behavior, and by consistently engaging in a more desirable one.

Stage 3: I win some, I lose some, but the struggle builds strength. I gain insight that helps me continue to improve.

Stage 4: My trajectory stabilizes; wins become more common.

Stage 5: Abstinence or adherence (depending on the goal) becomes increasingly "automatic."

Stage 6: Similar to how I suddenly noticed there was something I should change, I suddenly notice that I *have* changed. I've integrated the new habit into my identity, and the newly established "circuits" in my mind take care of the rest.

notes:_____

_____

_____

SINS, SINNERS, AND SUFFERING

(6)

The word "sin" conjures an image of a crime, an act that must be punished. But what if this image is wrong? What if *sin* would be better understood as "error?" And what if, by using the word *error*, we gain a more useful perspective? Take the seven deadly sins as an example: pride, lust, greed, gluttony, sloth, envy, wrath. They are errors because they lead to suffering—not in the afterlife, but here and now. The suffering isn't a punishment; it is simply an unavoidable consequence of the *error* we've embraced. And if we accept that perspective, we may discover other errors as well; fear, hatred, and judgement come immediately to mind.

(7)

I suffer when I sin; therefore, I suffer when I judge.

(8)

The goal is to acknowledge what is, without poisoning yourself with judgement and other forms of negative energy.

(9)

It's possible to explain that a person lies or cheats or steals or manipulates (or worse), without feeding something unhealthy in yourself. It's possible to acknowledge the reality of what they do, and acknowledge that it constitutes

notes:_____

_____

_____

unacceptable behavior, without filling yourself with self-righteous indignation. When dealing with dishonest and dangerous people, discernment and self-defense are always necessary, but celebrating assumed superiority is not.

(10)
Supremacism is driven by a common and pernicious human desire: to acquire status and the "right" to demean or dominate others. Ironically, it's not uncommon for supremacists to falsely accuse others of "supremacism" in order to signal, and satisfy their own lust for, supremacy.

(11)
Everyone enters this world with different errors to overcome. Defend yourself against the "dregs of humanity," but don't waste time pondering their moral inferiority. *Especially* when you see traits in them that, within your lifetime, once existed in you.

(12)
It is not my job to judge others. It is not my job to convince others *not to* judge me. However, it *is* my job to judge myself honestly and correct errors when I find them. That's where my focus belongs.

notes:_____

_____

_____

(13)

What if extremely annoying people and circumstances serve a purpose? What if that purpose is to teach you the benefits of becoming less easily annoyed?

(14)

Certain emotions deduct value from the quality of your life. Aggravation, hatred, depression, fear, etc. These emotions come at a high cost, and you're offered the opportunity to pay that cost on a daily basis. If you seek greater peace and happiness, you must learn to reject the offer. And if you're unable to reply with a firm no, you should insist on negotiating a discount. Ask yourself: "How could I view this situation so that my cost is 20% lower? How could I view this in such a way that it cuts my cost in half? Can I find a perspective that produces no cost at all?" And if you fail to reduce the initial intensity of the emotion, then cut your costs by limiting its duration. "How long should I accept this state of mind? Five more minutes? Five more hours? Five more days? Five more weeks? Five more years? Should I embrace and nourish this unhealthy state until the day I die, or should I find a better way?"

notes:_____

_____

_____

FINDING FULFILMENT

(15)
It's better to be laughed at for trying than to be accepted for not.

(16)
Healthy and unhealthy paths to fulfillment:
Healthy: establishing self-control.
Unhealthy: seeking to control others.
Healthy: a primary focus on becoming better than you are.
Unhealthy: a primary focus on being seen as "better than" others.
Healthy: cultivating a habit of gratitude.
Unhealthy: cultivating a habit of resentment.

(17)
We're born helpless and remain vulnerable for many years. As such, it's understandable that children establish a habit of approval-seeking behavior. But the habits of a child aren't sufficient to meet the needs of a healthy adult. Adults must mature beyond the fear of rejection. They must relinquish the need for constant reassurance and encouragement while strengthening their ability to endure the opposite.

(18)
A psychologically healthy person is not easily manipulated by praise or insults.

notes:_____

_____

_____

(19)

Whether you're fit or fat, strong or weak, black or white, tall or short, you will be judged. The clothes you choose, the music you like, the people you respect, the things you believe or don't believe—all of these will bring ridicule or praise depending on the spectator. For this reason, approval-seeking behavior is a foolish game. Learn to recognize and eliminate your errors ("know thyself"), and those who judge you will have an increasingly insignificant effect on your peace of mind.

(20)

If you really believe in what you're doing, the ridicule of others is no reason to stop. Likewise, if you despise what you're doing, the encouragement of others is a terrible reason to continue.

(21)

Let them think less of you. And while you're at it, don't waste your time thinking less of them; you'll only poison yourself with negative energy. Besides, it's foolish to expect others to see you the way you wish to be seen. Even if you could force them, you shouldn't; you have no right. So, let them think less of you. Don't waste your time thinking less of them, and taking it one step further, let them think more of themselves for whatever ridiculous reason they choose. To the extent they need to feel superior, they reveal their suffering, not their superiority. Don't pretend otherwise.

notes:_____

_____

_____

(22)

Want to make progress and feel empowered? Focus on things that are under your control. Want to stagnate and feel helpless? Focus on things that aren't.

(23)

Identify and eliminate the thoughts, feelings, and behaviors that weaken you. Identify and cultivate the thoughts, feelings, and behaviors that empower you. That's enough to keep you busy for a lifetime.

(24)

We were born with an immune system that protects our body from pathogens. Unfortunately, we *weren't* born with a psychological immune system. If we want to protect ourselves from pathogenic thoughts, we must develop psychological immunity on our own.

(25)

We get better at what we practice, for better or worse.

(26)

If we choose to embrace ugliness, we increase our ability to embrace it again. If we choose to reject ugliness, we increase our ability to reject it again. Either choice increases our ability; it's just a matter of deciding which ability we'd rather strengthen.

notes:_____

_____

_____

(27)

What will fulfill us more than anything in this life? Maybe we don't know, but we can probably guess what won't. Our greatest fulfilment won't come from anger or resentment or jealousy. It won't come from greed or lust or vengeance. It definitely won't come from fear, insecurity, or depression. So, if nothing else, maybe we should stop practicing these states of being. In their absence, we're likely to find something better.

(28)

Develop traits that can be improved for a lifetime: patience, honesty, compassion, humility, gratitude, determination, fearlessness, self-control, personal responsibility…You'll never run out of work or rewards.

(29)

Unfortunately, most of us overreact when confronted with minor inconveniences, disagreements, or rejection. It's foolish. With just a little effort, we can put things in a healthier perspective and dramatically improve our experience. Why not develop this skill? It's extremely valuable, especially when dealing with much bigger challenges.

(30)

Beneficial transformation can occur naturally over time, or it can occur through deliberate choice and effort. The deliberate

notes:_____

_____

_____

path is more reliable, and it leads to amazing benefits that last a lifetime.

(31)
Eliminating even a *single* self-destructive habit (like compulsive drinking, eating, shopping, gambling, judging, worrying, complaining, etc.) will have an enormous positive impact on the quality of your life.

(32)
"Be the change that you'd like to see in the world" is great advice, but avoid making it an unhealthy ego thing. Don't use your progress as an excuse to dehumanize "the others" who are unable or unwilling to change. (That ruins everything.) Instead, keep striving to become a healthier human, contribute what you feel compelled to contribute, and try to leave the people and things you touch a little better off than they were. That's all that can be expected, and in all honesty, it's one hell of an accomplishment.

(33)
Some high achievers seem obsessed with making others feel less than, whereas others convey no such desire. This illustrates how primary objectives matter. Are you primarily motivated to become your best and potentially inspire others in the process, or are you primarily motivated to intimidate others and prove you're better than them? I

notes:_____

_____

_____

believe the first requires self-confidence, and the latter is driven by insecurity.

PERSONAL EXPERIENCES, DREAMS, MEDITATIONS

(34)

While meditating last night, I went back in time to 1981. Rush's "Moving Pictures" album had only been out for a couple of weeks, and there I was standing in the living room of our two-bedroom apartment with my very own copy. I was 11 years old and couldn't wait to hear the entire album—again. So, as I'd already done a dozen times before, I carefully removed the album from its cover, put it on the turntable, dropped the needle, and cranked it up. Instant bliss.

Listening to *Tom Sawyer*, *Limelight*, *Red Barchetta*, *YYZ*, *The Camera Eye*; each song stirred amazing feelings in the 11-year-old child. Rush was on top of the world, and the member I identified with most (drummer and lyricist, Neil Peart) was in the prime of his life. Neil was 28 years old, touring the globe and living his dream. I held the vision of that moment in time and its euphoric feelings for a few minutes. Then, by simply changing my focus, I left the past and returned to the present moment...In an instant, 40 years

notes:_____

_____

_____

were gone, and my 28-year-old hero, Neil, had reached the age of 67 and then passed away.

I emerged with two thoughts: 1. Our physical lives, whether we live to 9 or 99, are short. Our trip will be over in the blink of an eye. 2. The boundless joy and enthusiastic energy of our youth is always available to us. We simply need to give ourselves permission to experience it again—perhaps by listening to an old song, remembering an old friend, or simply recognizing the profound gift and opportunity contained in each breath.

(35)

I struggled with serious bouts of depression for more than a decade and, like many depressed people, I considered it something that I just had to live with. Then, after a lot of unnecessary suffering, I finally figured out what was going on. I realized that I was doing it to myself; that a dysfunctional piece of my personality actually *wanted* to be depressed. It enjoyed the certainty of its hopeless perspectives, and it fed on negative energy. When this became clear (that a worthless circuit in my head was actively trying to create and sustain depression), I was able to isolate and attack it. From then on, it became progressively easier for me to recognize its voice. It became easier for me to say, in essence, "I'm not doing that to myself anymore. Fuck off." It wasn't about ignoring difficult challenges; it was about choosing less dramatic, healthier ways to respond.

notes:_____

_____

_____

(36)

I refuse to engage in approval-seeking behavior; it's not honest and it's not me. If somebody wants to think less of me for this (despite the fact that I haven't done anything wrong to them or even projected an ill thought in their general direction), they're perfectly within their right to do so. In fact, I prefer this to having them "like me" for pretending to be something I'm not.

(37)

I was a druggy, a liar, and a thief. I was a dangerous drunk, a cheater, and a bully. I hurt people. I wish it weren't true, but it is. Then, I stopped ignoring my conscience and, over a period of time, I became a different person. By age 16, I'd made a lot of progress. By age 21, I was no longer any of those things. The thought of weakening myself with drugs or alcohol disgusted me. The thought of lying, cheating, or stealing disgusted me. The thought of bullying somebody (trying to make a person feel less than) disgusted me. By learning to identify those thoughts as the enemy, I was able to destroy their influence. I believe everyone can do the same. I hope to help in some way.

notes:_____

_____

_____

HOW TO

(38)

Whenever a task (big or small) requires more effort than expected, it's easy to respond with impatience and aggravation. But does that response have any value? Does it help you in any way? Of course not. If you're struggling to get something done, there's only *one thing* that you need to focus on, one question that you need to ask: "**What is the next step?**" Keep asking and answering that question and you'll finish the task without needless suffering and wasted energy. Even if you decide that the next step is to temporarily (or permanently) stop trying, the same principle applies. That single question, "What is the next step?" fills the space that might otherwise fill up with impatience and aggravation. It diverts the mind away from idiocy and back toward a productive use of your energy.

(39)

"Do and observe." This is a story about a phrase I programmed into my mind in 2014. (Before I came up with "**What is the next step?**") Its purpose was to help me deal with a four-GPU-cryptocurrency mining rig that wouldn't stop crashing.

When I started the project, I figured it would only take about two or three hours to build the rig and get it running. Six hours later, I was still trying to get it going and I noticed two

notes:_____

_____

_____

intense points of stress. First, I felt stress prior to testing each new "fix" (because I desperately wanted the fix to work), and second, I felt stress each time the *fix* failed.

This repeating pattern of stress wasn't helping anything. Worse, it was draining me of the energy and focus I needed to figure out the problem. Fortunately, the idea of "letting go of the outcome" entered my mind, and it presented itself as a statement: "Do and observe."

Basically, "do and observe" meant that I could act with intent, but anything beyond that was out of my control. Do, observe, assess what *is* and then take the next step. Maybe this is what the gurus mean when they say, "Accept what is." *Acceptance,* in this context, doesn't mean "do nothing." It means "don't poison yourself with stress while deciding what to do," and certainly "don't poison yourself with stress when your attempted fix doesn't work." If you're committed to getting something done, "do and observe" until you *observe* the result you've set out to achieve, or until you decide to move on to something else.[3]

(40)
Don't ask if your response is justified; humans can justify almost anything. Don't ask if your response is normal; in a world gone mad, normal isn't an acceptable standard.

---

[3] For those who are wondering: one of the four GPUs was faulty. It wasn't until I decided to run the rig with different card configurations that I figured it out. My "two- to three-hour project" ended up taking about 13 hours total, but I got it done. From that day forward, the difficulties didn't matter. The rig was running/earning money; mission accomplished.

Instead, simply ask yourself: Is this response helpful? If the answer is no, focus less on what prompted the response, and focus more on how you can improve it.

GENERAL OBSERVATIONS

(41)
Either you're going to do the work or you're not. If you're going to do it, complaining about the process only drains energy that could be put to better use. If you're not going to do it, well, then you've got nothing to complain about.

(42)
Greatness comes in all shapes and sizes, colors, ages, and backgrounds. It discriminates only against those who expect it to be given rather than earned.

(43)
When it comes to dealing with problems, people usually choose between three options. Here they are, listed from best to worst:

Option 1: They relentlessly seek ways to improve or solve their problems. They begin with looking at how they might be causing or making problems worse, and they correct those errors.

notes:_____

_____

_____

Option 2: They pretend their problems don't exist. They hope their problems go away without requiring any change in behavior.

Option 3: They exploit each problem's ability to garner attention, diminished expectations, or perpetual "help" from others. They effectively convert their problems into an asset, a form of currency they use to acquire what they want.

Those who work to solve their problems inevitably become stronger, more independent, and develop a habit of not causing problems for themselves and others. Those who hope their problems go away without any effort will sometimes get lucky, but it's likely their bad problems will eventually get worse. Last but not least, those who choose to turn their problems into assets become weaker, less independent, and develop a habit of causing endless additional problems for themselves and others. The distance between the life they could have had and the life they end up with is enormous. They pay a terrible price.

notes:_____

_____

_____

SPIRITUAL

(44)

When I stopped embracing negative thoughts and energy, I gradually acquired the ability to explore and relate to spiritual ideas. (Meaning and purpose, loss of fear, a sense of connection to something greater; something eternal.) It wasn't intentional, it just happened. As if negativity and spirituality carry an opposite charge. Where one is firmly rooted in the mind, the other cannot go.

(45)

When it comes to health, spiritual is the most important form. It paves the way for all others and eases suffering in their absence.

(46)

Our spirit enters this world to overcome challenges that do not exist on the other side—challenges like hatred, fear, depression, insecurity, and craving. In the process of overcoming these, we gain spiritual strength that serves us here and beyond. Our progress is the one thing we get to take with us.

(47)

I understand the general concept, and I have no problem accepting that (in the end) "we're all one." I won't be

notes:_____

_____

_____

surprised at all to discover that, when we die, we shed our misinterpretations and once again experience our universal connectedness. In fact, I hope that's the case. However, I don't believe this means we should pretend that our physical and post-physical reality are the same. They're not. If they were the same, there'd be no point for us to be here.

On this physical side of existence, all living things are in differentiated form. The lion and gazelle are different. The serial killer and the healer are different. The abuser and the abused are different. Each are having very different experiences. Therefore, most people will intuitively, and rightfully, dismiss the guru who suggests "we're all the same; there is no difference." We might be inevitably heading toward that end, but we can't pretend we're already there. We have lessons to learn on this journey, and our differences are what provide us the opportunity to do so.

(48)
Every challenge provides an opportunity to prove fidelity to your conscience. I honestly believe that's the point of all this. It's less about winning the external battles (though we should certainly try). It's more about winning the inner battles, eliminating the errors that weaken and separate us from our higher selves. To the extent we make progress there, we're winning.

notes:_____

_____

_____

(49)

It's interesting to imagine that we choose the circumstances into which we're born. While thinking about that spiritual concept, I attempted to reconcile the difference between people who suffer as a result of poor life choices that they refuse to correct, versus those who suffer as a result of things beyond their control. In the case of those who suffer by choice, I can only assume they entered this life expecting to overcome the challenges they've encountered, but perhaps they underestimated the required level of commitment. It's OK, they'll get another chance. For the others, it's more complicated. Why would anyone choose to be born into suffering they couldn't do anything about? For instance, why would somebody choose to grow up as a Jew in 1920s Germany only to suffer and die in the Nazi concentration camps? If I were to imagine an answer, it would go something like this: Those who would choose to endure that level of suffering would only do so for the betterment of mankind, to show how fear and hate are used to obtain unrestrained power. To expose the inevitable consequences of allowing the seekers of unrestrained power to acquire it. They would do it to contribute to the evolution of human consciousness and to hopefully prevent *billions* from being enslaved, experimented on, starved, controlled, or killed in the future.

notes:_____

_____

_____

CHAPTER 2

The Inner Idiot

(1)

Let's start with a basic premise: Somewhere in your head, there's an unhealthy version of you that sucks. We'll call it your inner idiot. It's whiny, anxious, easily irritated, and compulsive. It wants to blame, complain, and judge. Ultimately, the inner idiot produces self-destructive thoughts, feelings, and behaviors because these are necessary for its survival. It feeds on negative energy, and so it manipulates you into producing its meals. Contrary to what the idiot would have you believe, your primary battle isn't against the outside world; it's against the idiot's attempt to monopolize your reactions.

(2)

When you feel yourself slipping into a state of intense anger, fear, depression, judgement, or craving, consciously acknowledge that some small part of you *WANTS* to enter that unhealthy state of being. Consider it your inner idiot, and *please* don't feel bad; everybody's got one. By identifying the idiot, you begin the process of limiting the amount of damage it can do.

notes:_____

_____

_____

(3)

Bad habits (mental and physical) *can* be conquered, but many people won't even try because they're too afraid they'll lose the fight. This fear is normal, but unnecessary. First, if a person hasn't developed the required circuits to overcome a bad habit *before* they attempt to eliminate it, they shouldn't be surprised if they come up short here and there. It's common. Second, even the "coming up short" part of the process *can be* used in a way that eventually leads to the desired change. It all depends on how they mentally process events that take place before, during, and after the "slip-up."

As an example, let's consider a hypothetical compulsive eater; we'll call her Sally. Sally has finally realized that her love of sweets is a problem, and she's also realized that she *should* alter her behavior. Unfortunately, she's currently home alone with her inner idiot, and the idiot is tempting her to get into the ice cream. What Sally hasn't realized is this: As long as she doesn't embrace and identify with the desire, she can still turn an ice-cream-eating incident into a win. As long as she doesn't say, "Screw it! I'm gonna eat the entire gallon of this chocolate chip, double fudge, cookie-crunch surprise, and I DON'T CARE! I LOVE ICE CREAM!" she can still weaken the compulsive desire. But how?

Well, once again, it *starts* with refusing to embrace and identify with the unwanted circuit that's creating the desire.

notes:_____

_____

_____

Sally needs to understand that she's been feeding that unhealthy circuit for years; it's still strong. But she also needs to understand that it's *not a fixed part* of who she is. Sally could just as easily feel disgusted by the idea of eating a gallon of ice cream. For instance, if she firmly associated the sugar in ice cream with metabolic poison—if she linked excessive sugar consumption to the chronic psychological pain of her obesity, the suffering caused by diabetes, and the incapacitating effects of premature aging—her desire to gorge herself with sugar (in the form of a gallon of ice cream), would be nonexistent. And, of course, that's the ideal outcome: *zero desire* to engage in self-destructive behavior.

But we've already established that Sally is new at this. She's still in the "win some, lose some" phase of overcoming her impulse to get into the chocolate chip, double fudge, cookie-crunch surprise. Today she has decided to *partially* indulge the urge. It's less than ideal, but it's OK. Here's how she can limit the damage and even gain some ground:

1) *Before* she begins, she establishes that *she* is in control of the decision, and she's going to attack/undermine the "idiot circuit" the entire time.

2) *During*, she does exactly that. She maintains her contempt for the unwanted desire. Her inner dialogue might go something like this: "OK, circuit, here we go. Let's eat a little

notes:_____

_____

_____

bit of this poisonous frozen sugar...Wow, tastes like diabetes, heart disease, and premature aging. How fantastic!" It sounds silly, but belittling an irrational/self-destructive circuit is infinitely more useful than enthusiastically embracing it as if it represents "you," only to hate yourself later for embracing it. And ending on that note:

3) *After* the event, Sally needs to make sure that she doesn't get conned into hating herself. Odds are, if she followed steps 1 and 2, she didn't eat anywhere near a gallon of ice cream, but even if she did, she needs to realize that hating herself is another inner-idiot-driven impulse. This is true for everyone. It's OK to hate the circuits/impulses, but don't let the idiot convince you that you *are* the circuits. You're not. You are the consciousness that can observe and change them. And with consistent, intelligently directed effort, that's exactly what you'll do.

(4)
The inner idiot, at its core, is self-destructive. It chases temporary pleasures and distractions that produce long-term pain.

(5)
I'm convinced the ruling class relies heavily on cultivating and manipulating the inner idiot in as many people as they possibly can. It enables them to exploit vulnerabilities in the

notes:_____

_____

_____

default human operating system. Fortunately, to the extent we raise our level of consciousness and overcome those vulnerabilities, we become far more difficult to manipulate and control via fear, hate, status seeking, resentment, depression, and self-destructive escapism.

(6)
Don't let the idiot drive.

SIN, SINNERS, AND SUFFERING

(7)
Lust produces insatiable desire. It is suffering disguised as pleasure. (Lust for money, fame, power, sex; it's all the same.) The solution to this suffering is to see lust for what it is and to acknowledge your role in creating it. In the simplest terms: You create lust by exaggerating the value of what you desire while simultaneously minimizing (or completely ignoring) the cost of worshiping it.

(8)
Despite presenting itself as the ultimate escape and path to pleasure, lust cultivates beliefs and behaviors that inevitably lead to suffering. Whether the aim is food, attention, power, sex or anything else, lust exaggerates the value of these things and, over time, enslaves the mind. Unchecked, the individual trades their long-term health and happiness for

notes:_____

_____

_____

short-term rewards—rewards that bring ever-decreasing pleasure and ever-mounting consequences.

(9)
Physical pain provides the most basic indication that you are doing something wrong. (Touch fire. It causes pain. You instinctively pull away.) But for some reason people never figure this out when it comes to psychological pain. The principle is the same: Pain provides an indication that you are doing something wrong (in this case, using your mind as a weapon against yourself). But people become attached to their psychological pain. They seem to cherish it. Their suffering becomes part of their identity, and they don't want to let it go. They not only "touch the fire" whenever possible, they douse themselves in gasoline prior to doing so.

(10)
Do *not* take pleasure in the suffering of others. If you feed that impulse, it will grow and eventually feed on you.

(11)
The victim personality gravitates toward bad choices because the subsequent hardships provide access to what they consciously, or unconsciously, desire: sympathy, attention, and assistance. It's a self-destructive path to power, often via guilt, over others.

notes:_____

_____

_____

(12)

Sympathy, like a drug, only makes problems *temporarily* more tolerable. It numbs the symptoms but leaves the *cause* of suffering intact. Worse, it actually encourages people to do nothing. It diverts their attention away from options that could improve or even solve their problems. In short, seeking sympathy, unlike seeking solutions, tends to prolong suffering and make things worse.

(13)

Some people equate sympathy with love, and that creates a perverse incentive (often unconscious) for them to avoid solving their problems.

(14)

There are necessary struggles that stem from the growing process. They're different from the unnecessary struggles that stem from refusing to grow.

FINDING FULFILMENT

(15)

The fundamental treasures of life cannot be borrowed, stolen, bartered, or bought. They are kept within and can only be earned.

notes:_____

_____

_____

(16)

Trying to control things that are outside of our control will always erode our confidence. In a social setting, this often boils down to wanting others to view us in a favorable way. We'd prefer to be seen as intelligent or funny or good looking or moral or talented or strong or tough, etc. What this really means is: We'd all prefer to be seen as desirable in some way. But that's out of our hands.

By all means, we should strive to make the most of ourselves and contribute our best, but always with the understanding that others will see and judge us as they see fit. That is their business, not ours. When we want everyone to see us as we wish to be seen, we are asking too much and we suffer for it. It's a problem that only we can solve. We do that by returning our focus to the *one* thing we *can* control: our reaction. But what does that look like in practice?

The first step is easy: We express gratitude when people view us in a favorable way. (You're probably doing that already.) The second step requires significantly more effort: We develop our ability to tolerate the negative opinion of others, just as they must develop the ability to tolerate our less-than-fantastic opinion of them. Although step two is more difficult, it's where real strength is developed. It not only forces us to respect the rights of others (which includes the

notes:_____

_____

_____

right to judge us negatively); it reminds us to avoid defining our value, high or low, based on their opinion.

(17)

If you can remain humble while receiving praise, you're halfway there. If you can remain humble while receiving insults, congratulations; you made it!

(18)

It's easy to feel gratitude when others appreciate you, but what about when they don't? What about when they unjustly disparage or outright lie about you or a group that you identify with? How can you find gratitude then? Admittedly, it's *much more* challenging, but it's still possible if you've done the work. (1), you can be grateful that the illness within them no longer has the power to provoke you. (2), you can be grateful that your peace of mind doesn't depend on something you simply can't control (what others think and say). (3), you can be grateful that you're not filled with ugliness and suffering like they are.

(19)

Have they lied about you? Have they mischaracterized who you are? Are you furious? If so, your peace of mind depends too much on the perception of others. There will always be

notes:_____

_____

_____

liars, and there will always be those who believe them, but honest and thoughtful people will see through and ignore them both.

(20)
If I take an insult personally, who does it harm?

(21)
Next time you're provoked into a state of anger or disgust— next time you feel an insatiable urge to vilify somebody— shift your focus to the energy within you. Look at it closely; you'll realize that it's pure poison. If there's any doubt, shift your focus again, this time to somebody who inspires love, gratitude, or a deep sense of admiration. Which energy would you like more of?

(22)
If you don't train your brain, it will behave like a reactionary idiot. Your first thought/response to daily provocations is rarely the best, and it's never the only option to choose from. Develop better responses and you'll eliminate an enormous amount of unnecessary suffering from your life.

(23)
Independent people are sometimes viewed as aloof, or worse, arrogant. It could simply be that they've recognized the foolishness of deriving their sense of self from the opinion

notes:_____

_____

_____

of others. If you think about it, chasing approval is a terrible waste of time. The average person can love you one second and then hate you the next based on the silliest of things. If you're not secure in who you are, that will lead to a very unstable emotional existence.

(24)
Arrogance is ugly, even when it's based on something *earned*. It's even uglier when it's based on something the person had nothing to do with.

(25)
If you're unaffected by the negative opinion of others, don't be surprised if they accuse you of arrogance. Also, don't expect them to recognize the irony. (The arrogance of suggesting that their opinion of you is more important than your own opinion of yourself.) When dealing with people like this, there's no reason to let them under your skin. Assuming you treat people with respect, odds are the "problem" has more to do with them than you.

(26)
The wise focus on becoming better. The unwise focus on becoming "better than."

notes:_____

_____

_____

PERSONAL EXPERIENCES, DREAMS, MEDITATIONS

(27)

I had another extremely profound experience today. I've been taxing my mind with many different things the past week, not the least of which involves this final push to get my mom off psych meds/SSRIs. (They're literally destroying her mind.) I decided that the MOST IMPORTANT THING I COULD DO to get myself back to feeling normal was to do *nothing*. So, I turned off the air purifier, turned off all but a couple of lights, opened the door (so I could hear the bugs), and sat down on the couch to stare at our sandstone-block wall and fireplace. It was 10:10 p.m.

Within a few minutes I started to feel a slight bit of disorientation and uncomfortable awareness. Not as freaky as when I woke up in Cleveland and had no idea *what* I was, let alone *where* I was or what I was looking at, and not as bad as the comparably disturbing experience in New Hampshire when I woke up and, looking at the TV, felt like I was staring at an exploded diagram of its molecular structure—nothing like that. But a feeling of slipping into a disassociated mental space was there, and it was unsettling. Fortunately, I managed to just observe the state (without scrambling mentally to regain my bearings), and that allowed the experience to present itself as a concept: like it was a higher

notes:_____

_____

_____

form of awareness "coming online" and struggling a bit to get acclimated. That idea made it easier for me to "get out of the way" and, once the awareness settled in, the experience changed completely. I could see or almost *feel* my brain rewiring…reorganizing. As if the dendrites were all moving around, forming new, healthier connections to perceive and erase errors. The slight anxiousness (brought on by initial disorientation) had disappeared, and I was suddenly just present. It was *truly* amazing.

For nearly an hour and a half, I simply stared at the wall, listened to the bugs, listened to Rocko snoring…and it was like being nourished or renewed. Not once did I feel any desire to think about anything that I "had to do" or anything I "had to make a decision on." Somebody could have handed me 10,000 dollars or 10 million dollars, and it wouldn't have had any effect; it wouldn't have increased the incredible sense of peace and gratitude that I was feeling. I needed *nothing*.

Nearing the end, Rocko woke up and rolled over on his back (his way of requesting attention). I got off the couch, laid face to face with him on the floor, scratched his chest, and while looking at his upside-down face (lips flopped back, revealing a beautiful doggy grin), I realized something. As long as I remind myself to do this from time to time—to simply sit and connect with peace and presence— I'm going to be just fine.

notes:_____

_____

_____

HOW TO

(28)

Don't be fooled. The inner idiot is simply a maladaptive network of neurons that you've unconsciously created. (It's not you.) If the idiot is causing you sufficient harm, it can and should be evicted from your mind. Begin by interrupting its energy. Stop feeding it. Stop identifying with its errors. Your brain will get the message and initiate the "pruning" process.

(29)

It's important to occasionally measure your progress. Regarding unwanted reactions, there are three areas that are worth looking at:

1. the frequency of the unwanted reaction
2. the intensity of the unwanted reaction, and
3. the duration of the unwanted reaction

In the past, were you provoked multiple times per day and now it only happens a few times per week? Did the intensity of the unwanted reaction reach level 10 in the past, but now it rarely exceeds a 5? Would an unwanted reaction normally occupy your mind for hours or even days, but now you can get over it much more quickly? Whatever the improvements

notes:_____

_____

_____

are, it's important to recognize the progress you're making and allow yourself to feel gratitude. Even if there is still a lot of ground to cover, your **trajectory is what matters**. Never let the *inner idiot* convince you otherwise.

(30)

Your reactions are the only thing you can develop real control over, so learn to catch yourself when they go wrong. Learn to say, "I *refuse* to use this as an excuse to poison myself. I refuse to feed anger, resentment, anxiety, or depression because they only make *me* suffer." Then, *as soon as you're able*, reassert your control over the present moment. Shift your focus toward the innumerable things that you *can* be grateful for (things that are far more important than whatever triggered you). It's like a muscle that has to be developed, but once that new muscle gets strong, it will change your perception of yourself. You'll realize that you're much more powerful than you formerly believed.

(31)

When people are feeling ungrateful, they're often told to list things that they *should be* grateful for. The problem is when you're in a deeply ungrateful state of mind, it's difficult to generate any sincerity or positive emotion while writing the list. So, next time, try some reverse psychology.

notes:_____

_____

_____

When ungrateful energy has you in its grip, instead of writing a list of things you *should* be grateful for, make a list of things that you are *choosing* NOT TO be grateful for. It works because it allows you to maintain your ungrateful/negative state while simultaneously revealing its absurdity.

Your list can include anything: "Right now, I don't care that I've got plenty to eat" (imagine an empty refrigerator, empty kitchen cabinets, and no money to buy food). "I don't care that I currently have a roof over my head and a warm bed to sleep in" (imagine living on the streets without shelter). "I don't care that I've got two arms and legs" (imagine trading places with Nick Vujicic), etc.

This thought experiment makes it easier to weaken the ungrateful circuit pretending to be you. Clearly, you *do* care that you're not starving, homeless, wet and cold, or that you aren't forced to overcome the challenges of living without arms and legs. And if the inner idiot insists that you're *not* grateful for any of these things, take a moment to really imagine one month of hunger or one year of homelessness or a lifetime without your limbs. Odds are the real you will shut the idiot down in a hurry.

notes:_____

_____

_____

GENERAL OBSERVATIONS

(32)

There's nothing wrong with choosing a path that leads to suffering. There's nothing wrong with remaining on that path until the day you die. What's wrong is the idea that you're not capable of choosing another path.

(33)

Intense pain indicates improper action. (Physical or mental.)

(34)

For better or worse, we absorb thought patterns and behaviors from those around us. If you grew up with psychologically healthy/well-adjusted people, you're probably doing alright. If you grew up surrounded by lunacy (like most of us), you've probably got some work to do.

(35)

It's one thing to identify a circuit that needs to be reprogramed, but it's another thing entirely to get it done. Like exercise, knowing what you need to do isn't enough. You have to do the work.

(36)

The harder you work to acquire something, the more strength you'll develop to keep it.

notes:_____

_____

_____

(37)

Negative emotions are earned. How you direct your mind determines how much of each you're paid.

(38)

Best case scenario, you consciously program your automatic mind to serve your healthiest and highest self. Worst case scenario, your automatic mind is programmed by others, and you mistake the programs for who you are.

(39)

School struck me as an attempt to teach one primary lesson over and over again: "Do and say what the teacher tells you, and you'll never be wrong; do or say something else, and you'll never be right." It was that simple. All incentives were stacked on the side of blind obedience, and all punishments were reserved for those who refused to cooperate. I was punished often. It was worth it.

(40)

It's not where you launch; it's where you land that counts.

(41)

ONE useful thought that you choose to act on can dramatically improve your life.

notes:_____

_____

_____

(42)

When all is said and done, only one thing will matter: Did you disobey your demons, or did you empower them?

(43)

As you increase your level of awareness, the fool within has fewer and fewer places to hide.

SPIRITUAL

(44)

The spiritual path begins with calmly and patiently observing the unhealthy inner voice. As we learn to notice it, the process of disassociation begins. We start to see the difference between the voice and the peaceful awareness that observes it. In that moment of awareness, we not only experience what we are, we simultaneously identify what we're not. The chattering is pushed out, and it takes our unnecessary suffering with it.

(45)

Spirituality opens new realms of consciousness. It connects us to something greater, something ageless, something infinite. It eases suffering. It imparts strength and understanding. Best of all, we needn't work to develop spirituality. We simply need to eliminate the characteristics that obstruct it.

notes:_____

_____

_____

(46)

While lying down for my nap today, I suddenly heard a booming voice in my head. I didn't realize that I'd fallen asleep, and because so, it startled me. For a split second, I thought, "Is this what a person with schizophrenia experiences?" Immediately following that thought, I snapped out of the semiconscious dream state, and my focus shifted to the four words that I'd heard. "You **KNOW** it's true." It was like somebody beamed an audible answer directly into my brain. Next, I remembered the question I'd been thinking about before I drifted off: Does our consciousness survive physical death?

(47)

After having a near-death experience, survivors often return with the same message: Death isn't what you think it is; it's nothing to fear or mourn. Our consciousness does *not* require a body to exist; it survives physical death. Lastly, they inform us that the suffering of this world is only *temporary*; the indescribable peace that we return to is ageless…eternal.

(48)

I can't prove that consciousness survives physical death any more than somebody else can prove that it doesn't. However, I know that profound experiences have led me to believe that it does, and this belief has added immeasurable value to the quality of my life.

notes:_____

_____

_____

(49)

If you could choose your dreams prior to going to sleep (and experience them as reality), what type of dreams would you choose? Would you only choose pleasurable experiences, or would you choose difficult experiences as well? What if you knew that difficult experiences in your dreams would lead to deep insights, greater strength, and spiritual growth when you woke up?

With that in mind, take the question a step further. If you could choose your *experiences* prior to entering this life, what type of experiences would you choose? What if you knew that difficult experiences would lead to deep insights, greater strength, and spiritual growth when you "woke up" from this dream that we call life?

notes:_____

_____

_____

CHAPTER 3

The Ego

(1)

When most people hear the word "ego," they automatically associate it with something negative. This is unfortunate because ego isn't all bad. Think of ego as the collection of thoughts and beliefs that a person has incorporated into their identity. Many of the thoughts and beliefs are neutral, some of them are positive, and, of course, some of them might be negative.

To illustrate, imagine there's a man named Pete. "Pete" didn't know his name was Pete when he was born, but over the years he came to accept that name as part of his identity. Therefore, the name Pete is part of Pete's ego, but it's completely neutral.

Now, imagine that Pete became interested in helping sick children. At the age of 18 he started a nonprofit organization, and, 20 years later, his organization raises millions annually. Pete thinks of himself as a "nonprofit founder who's dedicated his life to helping children." These ideas are also

notes:_____

_____

_____

part of his ego/identity, but they're not neutral; they're actually positive.

Ok, we've covered neutral and positive; now we need an example of Pete's *negative* egoic thoughts and beliefs. But even this might play out differently than most would assume. Does Pete consider himself better than people who don't share his priorities in life? (No.) Does he feel jealousy when a less principled organization gets more media coverage and raises more money? (No.) Does he expect a fawning show of appreciation from those he helps? (Not at all.)

The negative egoic belief that Pete suffers from is that nothing he can do will ever be good enough, and that too many children are suffering because of his inadequacy. This is an especially destructive form of negative ego because few recognize that it's a problem. In fact, many believe the opposite. They view it as proof of humility and therefore healthy and *good*. (It's not.)

In the examples given, Pete only needs to get this final part of his ego in check. He can do that by first removing "inadequate" from the list of words he identifies with. Next, he should replace that word and its implications with a healthier assessment of his impact on the world. Perhaps he could acknowledge that he wants to do much more, but in the meantime, "far fewer children are suffering as a result of

notes:_____

_____

_____

the work that he and others have managed to get done." He could go further by adding, "And we're 100% committed to doing more in the future." This creates gratitude for what *is* and *can be* done, instead of creating ingratitude for what isn't or can't be. The former nourishes health within the ego; the latter creates illness.

(2)
Ego – The ideas that you've accepted about who you are. These accepted ideas can be accurate or inaccurate, productive or counterproductive. Regardless of their value, because you identify with them, they determine how you respond to the challenges of life. They inform your reactions and behavior to such a degree that even one improvement can produce enormous benefits.

(3)
When our physical body is ill, we do not assume the body itself is the problem (we make a distinction between the illness and the body). Well, we should do the same with the ego. Just like our physical body, our ego can become ill. The ego itself isn't bad; the illness that's affecting it is. And by framing it this way in our mind, we can begin the process of treating the problem. We can sever the illness from our accepted identity, and, by employing two things that comprise the ego's immune system (self-awareness and a willingness to change), we can restore its health.

notes:_____

_____

_____

(4)

If a person sits on a couch for five years eating nothing but ice cream and doughnuts, drinking nothing but Pepsi, Dr. Pepper, milkshakes, and beer, their body will become very unhealthy. However, nobody will ever suggest that "the body is the problem; we must kill it!" So, why then do people recommend "killing the ego" when it has endured an equivalent level of abuse? The ego itself isn't the problem. It's simply expressing disease caused by a steady diet of horribly unhealthy ideas. It's expressing disease caused by an appalling lack of anything approximating "nourishment" for the mind. If unhealthy elements of the ego have become troublesome, the answer isn't "kill the ego." The answer is "help the ego recover its health."

SIN, SINNERS, AND SUFFERING

(5)

If your ego is unhealthy, you'll spend a great deal of time focused on the differences between you and "others." It won't matter if the differences are based on how incredibly awesome you are or how incredibly inferior you are. When afflicted, the ego's only goal is to determine your place in its imagined hierarchy of superiority. It might even offer you the distinction of being *superior to others* based on your level of suffering. It might declare you a gold medalist in the suffering Olympics! My advice? Heal your ego. Focus on becoming healthier; forget about vying for status.

notes:_____

_____

_____

(6)

Unfortunately, most "debate" these days isn't about sharing information; it's about publicly shaming and belittling anyone who has a different point of view. It's a lower-ego thing. ("You're a monster and an idiot. Shut up, loser. I'm better than you.") If we could fix that, the odds of people listening to each other, and even admitting they "got something wrong," would go up dramatically. And the world would be a better place for it.

(7)

We've all seen it. The "good cause" that somebody claims to be fighting for isn't really about the cause. It's more about signaling their moral superiority. The cause is simply a path to status. It provides a right to posture. A right to belittle others in self-righteous indignation.

(8)

Status-seeking behavior ultimately aims at the acquisition of "stature" in the eyes of others. But if it depends entirely on the opinion of others, it's not stature. It's servitude.

(9)

Unopposed, the lower self will seek to establish its superiority over other human beings, and it will crush your higher self in the process.

notes:_____

_____

_____

(10)

Fixed attributes provide no indication of a person's honesty or integrity, no measure of their talent or creativity. Fixed attributes reveal nothing about a person's courage, their work ethic, or what their time on this planet will ultimately yield for the good of humanity. Those who ignore this fact, in my opinion, do so because they wish to elevate themselves above others without actually expending any effort of their own. They seek "superiority" as their birthright, but they end up demonstrating the opposite.

(11)

For some, it's only about pointing at others and screaming, "I'm a good person; you're not!" Whatever cause they choose to justify their superiority is secondary to the primary objective of putting themselves above you.

(12)

More often than not, people falsely equate tearing others down with making themselves bigger.

notes:_____

_____

_____

FINDING FULFILMENT

(13)
Your first responsibility is to take care of the body and brain you were given. You must breathe and sleep, you shouldn't eat or drink things that are poisonous, avoid beating yourself in the face with a hammer, etc. These are obvious, but another part of taking care of your body and brain involves paying attention to the things you focus on, and, more importantly, it involves paying attention to how you let those things affect you. If you're constantly filled with anger and resentment, you can't blame the world for that. Political systems and "the mob" have always been a mess. Try to keep in mind that many have endured unimaginable injustice and still managed to live grateful and productive lives. That was only possible because they refused to use their mind against themselves.

(14)
Recognize and accept responsibility for all of the negative thoughts and feelings that you experience—***all*** of them. By doing so, you turn your focus inward where it belongs.

(15)
It's pretty simple really: Allow yourself to love something and make a note of how you feel. Then, allow yourself to hate and do the same. Choose the feeling you want to experience most often and develop your mind accordingly.

notes:_____

_____

_____

(16)

When it comes to your problems, they might not be your fault, but they *are* your responsibility.

(17)

You must choose how to define yourself. No matter how terrible the circumstances, never choose the word "victim."

(18)

The negative consequences of our mental and behavioral habits may be very small at first. It's understandable how a person could think there's no problem and never think about it again. Knowing this, we'd be wise to periodically reexamine the consequences of our habits. If we look, we might realize they've become more obvious, and significantly more odious, with the passing of time.

(19)

Is a child more likely to be patient or impatient? Cautious or reckless? Confident or envious? Is a child more likely to possess or to lack self-discipline? Consider these questions when thinking about the elements of your personality and behavior that you'd like to change. How many of these elements formed decades ago, before you were old enough to see the potential consequences?

notes:_____

_____

_____

(20)

Self-destructive thoughts and behaviors serve a purpose: They nourish the self-destructive pieces of identity that exist within you. Remove those self-destructive pieces, and you'll be disgusted by the thoughts and behaviors you were formerly drawn to.

(21)

"Achieving" in an attempt to project significance or status over others versus achieving with hope to inspire and experience the joy of becoming more. The first leads to suffering; the other leads to fulfillment.

(22)

You're not less capable when people say you can't, and you're not more capable when they say you can. Dwelling on outside opinions is a waste of time. If you really want to know what you are or aren't capable of, get busy and find out.

(23)

The happiest people optimize for intrinsic reward. It's not that outward recognition doesn't yield an additional benefit for them; it does. It's just that the outward recognition isn't necessary.

notes:_____

_____

_____

(24)

Only you can decide what is and isn't right for you. It's a learning process, and it's not particularly easy. So, pursue what you *think* you want until it becomes clear that another path makes more sense. Take what you've learned and start again. As long as you're making honest choices (and honestly assessing the costs and rewards), progress is inevitable.

(25)

Let's say that you've had an argument with Bob. Bob gets mad and hurls a couple insults your way, but you manage to maintain your cool. Over the next few days, Bob practically exhausts himself reliving the argument. He tortures himself by imagining wild scenarios that lead to more conflict, he complains about you to anyone who'll listen, and the stress keeps him up at night. You, on the other hand, use the incident as an opportunity to *weaken* whatever remains of your unhealthy egoic impulses. You calmly explain the regrettable incident to anyone who asks. Who suffers less? Who gains more?

(26)

Never blame others for how they affect you. Choose your best response, own it, and if it's unhealthy, develop the ability to do better. You'll disarm the outside world and empower yourself in the process.

notes:_____

_____

_____

(27)

Your reaction to life is the one thing that you can develop real control over, and it's probably the greatest power you can possess. (It contributes to the acquisition and development of all others.) Regardless of the negative circumstances or challenges, don't use them as an excuse to weaken yourself with harmful energy. To the best of your ability, resist the urge; find a healthier perspective. It will be tough at first, but the long-term benefits are profound.

PERSONAL EXPERIENCES, DREAMS, MEDITATIONS

(28)

February 25, 2018, listening to Eckhart Tolle's book *A New Earth*. I'm *really* happy to hear him discuss the problem of people complaining or gossiping about others. He does a good job of capturing how some do this in an attempt to raise their own stature. Their complaints are more about signaling their superiority than trying to raise awareness about, or improve, any particular issue. The only problem I have is that he pins this on the ego in the same way that most spiritual leaders do (providing little or no clarification that the ego isn't always bad).

At this point in my life, I've rejected the idea that ego itself is bad. While listening to his characterization, my

notes:_____

_____

_____

mind immediately presented a few instances where my ego moved me toward healthier behavior. Example: It was my ego (sense of "separate self/identity") that prompted me to stop judging others in the way that Tolle describes because I realized I was only feeding something unhealthy within me, and poisoning myself with negative energy in the process. It was my ego/identity that believed I could "do better" than I was when my life consisted of doing drugs, lying, stealing, wasting away in jail, etc. It is my ego that views monogamy in my marriage as imperative and cheating as the most ridiculous/self-destructive thing I could do to harm my sense of self, not to mention the harm it would do to my wife and the life we share.

So basically, I just don't accept that ego is always bad, let alone unnecessary. I believe it exists for a reason and can work in conjunction with the higher self. That said, I realize that I might be misinterpreting what he and other spiritual leaders mean when they only refer to ego in a negative light.

(29)
Decades ago, I concluded that dishonesty weakens me. That was enough. So, to clarify, I don't demand honesty from myself as a way to gain respect from others. (I'm not even sure honesty matters to *most* people. If honesty is convenient, they're honest. If it's not convenient, they lie.)

notes:_____

_____

_____

Also, honesty isn't a moral-posturing thing for me. Who am I to say, "Honesty is the best policy"? It *is* for me; might not be for somebody else. (When I realize somebody can't be trusted, I treat their future statements and my relationship with them accordingly. No need to get indignant about it.) Finally, I don't demand honesty from myself out of some sense of obligation...Well, I guess that's not entirely true. I do feel somewhat "obligated" to obey my conscience because it's what led me out of all the terrible places that my dishonesty led me into. It seems like a reasonable way to show my appreciation.

(30)
While cutting the grass today, I imagined what it would be like to restore/rekindle the energy and enthusiasm of childhood. Then, an idea occurred to me: It isn't about restoring anything. The energy and enthusiasm are still there; they're simply buried beneath the filters you've picked up over the decades. It isn't about "adding" something back; it's about removing things that you've added.

(31)
My progress began when I accepted responsibility for what I was doing wrong.

notes:_____

_____

_____

HOW TO

(32)

The most important characteristics of a human being are found in people of every color. They are found in people who are gay or straight, fit or fat, short or tall. They are found in the religious and unreligious alike. The most important characteristics have little to do with beauty, intelligence, creativity, talent, wealth, or popularity. If you're not sure what they are, it isn't difficult to discover them: Be patient with yourself and others. Strive to help rather than harm. Practice understanding, love, honesty, and courage whenever you can; avoid judgement, hatred, deceit, and fear. By doing so, you'll discover, embody, and experience them for yourself.

(33)

Repeat after me: "I don't get to choose how others think or behave. I *DO* get to choose how they affect me."

(34)

I've always been uncomfortable with the way law-of-attraction types frame "the secret" to visualizing and manifesting goals. Although I agree that it's important to clearly see and feel what you want, the process is often presented in a troublesome way. It comes off as "just walk around like you've already got it, and you're all set!" This can generate all sorts of problems, not the least of which is a

notes:_____

_____

_____

mindset that takes the accomplishment for granted, a mindset that's not prepared to exert significant additional effort.

To avoid this issue, I'd describe a good visualization process like this: Imagine it's the day *after* you've achieved your goal. You wake up in the morning, open your eyes, and immediately remember that you've done it. A wave of relief and joy runs through you; you're so grateful that it practically hurts. Now, spend a few minutes experiencing that moment. Allow your nervous system to really soak in how good it feels. This creates a powerful imprint in your mind. Every cell within you will conclude: "Yes, this is a state that I want to live my life in." The greater the intensity, the easier it will be to add behaviors that move you closer, and weaken or eliminate behaviors that divert you.

(35)
Make a habit of nurturing higher states of mind, and higher states become the norm. Make a habit of nurturing lower states of mind, and lower states become the norm. Every moment of every day provides an opportunity to choose the level of consciousness that you cultivate and live in.

(36)
A negative habit of mind can only create negative narratives, feelings, and impulses. So, before taking it too seriously, know what you're dealing with. The habit is biased; it

notes:_____

_____

_____

exaggerates the significance of everything bad, ignores the significance of everything good, and it wastes your time with nonsense. Even if it temporarily hijacks your awareness, maintain your rightful contempt. Don't embrace or surrender to its unhealthy narratives.

(37)
Run when you can run, walk when you can walk, and crawl if that's the best you can do. Just keep moving in the right direction.

GENERAL OBSERVATIONS

(38)
Practice makes progress.

(39)
We can't do much about dishonesty and cowardice in others, so it's best that we attend to our own.

(40)
A slave to fear, a slave to those who create it;
a slave to lust, a slave to those who can provoke it;
a slave to gluttony, a slave to those who can facilitate it;
a slave to status, a slave to those who can bestow or revoke it;
a slave to nothing, a slave to no one.

notes:_____

_____

_____

(41)

Everyone does the best they can, given the strengths and weaknesses they've chosen to develop.

(42)

The education that matters most is the one that helps you achieve your goals. You can learn some basics in school, but be prepared to learn your greatest lessons elsewhere.

(43)

Success is what happens just before persistence fails.

(44)

More than luck, more than fate, our lives are the sum of our habitual thoughts and decisions.

(45)

The sincerity of your interest will determine the duration of your effort.

(46)

What benefit are "riches" that do not meet our deepest needs? What harm is there in "poverty" if within we are fulfilled?

(47)

The only thing worse than giving somebody false hope is filling them with false hopelessness.

notes:_____

_____

_____

(48)
Just because it's "normal" doesn't mean it's not a form of illness that ought to be treated.

(49)
Having a high IQ doesn't guarantee that you'll make good decisions in life, and it certainly doesn't guarantee that all of your conclusions are superior. Test-taking intelligence isn't the same as real life, problem-solving intelligence. Best I can tell, the latter is vastly superior, and it has little to do with a high number on an IQ test. Humility, patience, courage, honesty, and a sincere self-directed desire to learn (all of which can be developed and strengthened by anyone) yield superior results.

SPIRITUAL

(50)
Yes, you could say that the ego is the source of all suffering, but you could just as accurately say that the brain is the source of all suffering. Though technically true, it doesn't mean you should destroy the brain. Sure, you'll no longer be suffering, but you'll also no longer be in physical form.

(51)
The provocations we encounter, perceived as good or perceived as bad, are necessary. They are the catalyst for our

notes:_____

_____

_____

growth. They provide us an opportunity to choose a reaction, ranging from excellent to horrible, healthy to deadly. The more we move toward health, the closer we come to remembering who we are, why we're here, and what we're capable of.

(52)

If you had a time machine that enabled you to visit a deceased loved one for a few minutes every day, would you choose to visit their funeral? Or, instead, would you choose any of the countless wonderful times that you shared together? If the latter, why not do the same when it comes to choosing the time you spend *remembering* those you've lost? Why not spend quality time visiting with them, and be grateful that you can? Why not remember that those beautiful moments are always there to experience again? You simply need to choose them.

(53)

When I think of those who've contributed so much happiness to my life (those who are no longer here), I feel a deep sense of gratitude, not grief. I know that all of those years we spent together have left me immeasurably richer, not poorer. I know that I didn't "lose" them, because they were never mine to lose.

Everything that I love is on loan, including every cherished relationship. When I accept that, and when I can say, "You

notes:_____

_____

_____

gave me so much. THANK YOU!" (without expecting anything more) I'm able to connect with them in a way that doesn't hurt at all. And, oddly enough, I'm left with the sense that they haven't gone anywhere. They're still with me, still giving, if I only choose to see.

notes:_____

_____

_____

CHAPTER 4

Programming

(1)
Like it or not, your brain creates *programs* that automate your thinking and behavior. This being the case, the most important question to ask is: Do you understand and accept your role in the programming process? If you do, congratulations. As time passes, you'll get progressively better at monitoring, deleting, and writing new programs that serve you. However, if you don't understand and accept this responsibility, you'll be leaving the quality of your programs and your life to chance. You'll be more easily programmed and triggered by people who don't have your best interests in mind. You'll be more easily programmed and triggered by circumstances that are beyond your control. Worst of all, you'll mistake the compulsive thoughts, feelings, and behaviors of bad programming for "who you are."

(2)
I've said that the program "wants to be angry." Perhaps it would be better to say the program is designed to create

notes:_____

_____

_____

anger. It's simply looking for an opportunity to do its job. (The same could be said of a program that creates fear, lust, envy, insecurity, judgement, depression, etc.)

(3)
It's worth repeating. You have one very important job in this life: Recognize that *YOU* are the programmer, not the programs. You are the one who can identify undesirable circuits in your brain and, through deliberate conscious effort, weaken and replace them.

(4)
When you create a strong mental image of who you'd prefer to be, you simultaneously create a new circuit in your mind. That new circuit begins to compete with harmful circuits that used to have free reign over your thoughts and behavior. From that point forward, whenever an older/ harmful circuit is triggered, your mind will notice the conflict; it will "pause." In that moment, you'll be provided the opportunity to identify the unwanted circuit, mark it for deletion, and redirect your energy into a healthier one.

(5)
Imagine the following possibility: You acquired some unhealthy mental programs when you were young and, as you grew older, you integrated those programs into your identity. This made them stronger. Now, years or decades

notes:_____

_____

_____

later, the same programs continue to control how you react to certain provocations in the world. They limit you. They respond at the level of understanding that originally created them. Allowing them to persist puts you at risk—akin to occasionally giving a child control of your mind. At best, it's ill advised. At worst, it can ruin your life.

(6)

We hear of childhood wounds that need to be healed. Some people have a hard time relating to that concept; perhaps this is easier: Mental programs that you picked up in childhood can persist indefinitely. (It depends on how often they're used and how powerful they become.) If the programs are simple and beneficial (brush your teeth, wash your hands, don't pick your nose in public), it's not a problem. However, if the programs are emotionally charged and require greater maturity to resolve (feelings of abandonment, betrayal, abuse, fear, insecurity, etc.), it *is* a problem. If you don't replace/update those programs, you'll continue reacting at the level of consciousness that created them, regardless of your chronological age. You will struggle and suffer *unnecessarily*.

(7)

Perhaps the self-destructive program produces something dear to you. Perhaps you feel that erasing it is akin to erasing a piece of who you are. To be fair, if you've embraced the

notes:_____

_____

_____

program and its desires, you're somewhat correct. You *are* erasing a piece of your habitual identity, but it's a piece that's not worth keeping. It's a piece that can only lead to suffering, a piece that impedes your ability to experience a *more* fulfilling life.

SIN, SINNERS, AND SUFFERING

(8)

Everyone has problems, but those who acquire a taste for sympathy have no incentive to solve them.

(9)

They're miserable, and they *need* you to know it. When their problems bring you down, it makes them feel good. It's proof that somebody cares and, like a drug, it temporarily distracts them from straightening out the mess in their head. It solves nothing, but that's OK. They're not looking for solutions. They crave sympathy and attention; problems are the currency that help them acquire both. Their mind perfects its ability to produce misery because that's where the "rewards" are.

(10)

Through victimhood, they see a path to what they crave: attention, sympathy, or even supremacy—a "right" to dehumanize and disrespect others.

notes:_____

_____

_____

(11)

Think of *craving* or *lust* as an energetic parasite that infects a person's identity. Regardless of aim (attention, power, money, sex, etc.), the parasite emerges to feed and strengthen itself whenever possible. At the slightest provocation, it hijacks the mind and behavior of its host. Each time the individual embraces their craving/lust, they deepen its roots and power in the process. However, the opposite is also true. Once the individual sees craving/lust as an energetic parasite, it can no longer hide in the identity. By refusing to embrace it, the individual disrupts the nourishment it needs; it begins to weaken. The less it's fed, the sooner it dies.

(12)

Most self-destructive behaviors are driven by a false belief. "If I do this, it will ease my suffering." It won't. Yes, self-destructive behaviors temporarily distract you from something that ought to be dealt with, but the longer the distraction works, the bigger the unresolved problem gets.

(13)

The functional capacity of your brain and body can be improved or weakened based on how you choose to direct your energy. You can use your energy to reshape and strengthen your muscles, or you can use your energy to hammer nails into your feet. You can use your energy to reshape and strengthen your mind, or you can use your energy to poison it with substance

notes:_____

_____

_____

abuse, crappy food, chronic negativity, and vice. It's a choice. Each time you choose to improve functional capacity, you create a strength that spreads into other areas of your life. Likewise, if you choose to direct your energy unwisely, you create a weakness that produces harm across the board.

(14)

Trading an immediate sense of gain for an inevitable, long-term loss. Trading a moment of perceived pleasure for inevitable, long-term suffering. It's nothing more than a devil's bargain.

FINDING FULFILMENT

(15)

Here's a simple and effective philosophy: Do less of what makes the problems worse, and do more of what makes the problems better.

(16)

Gratitude for what you have *AND* for what you've had equals happiness. Resentment for what you never had *OR* no longer have equals misery.

(17)

There's no beauty requirement to be an excellent parent,

notes:_____

_____

_____

scientist, author, inventor, musician, spouse, comedian, actor, artist, entrepreneur, podcaster, fighter, doctor, trainer, speaker, business owner, consoler, nurse (the list goes on and on). So, ask yourself: What other socially exalted attributes are completely unnecessary for the development of excellence? Better yet, if you're lacking one or more of them, just fill in the blanks to see how much it matters.

There is no _____ requirement to be an excellent _____.

(18)
If there is fear, your mind created it. If there is anger, your mind created it. If there is resentment, insecurity, depression, or any other negative emotion, your mind created it as a response to something. But why?

Is it possible that the negative response is unnecessary? Is it possible that another person could face the same thing with far less suffering, or none at all? Is there any reason to avoid seeking a less-harmful perspective?

To clarify, I'm not suggesting negative emotions have no value; they do. Negative emotions indicate we're perceiving something in a harmful way, especially when we ratchet those emotions to the highest degree. What you feel in that moment is similar to the pain response from placing your hand in a fire—it's nature's way of telling you to alter your approach.

notes:_____

_____

_____

(19)

The keys to achieving something greater than temporary happiness:

1. Develop the ability to recognize and appreciate all that you've been given.
2. Develop the ability to recognize and appreciate all that you've earned.
3. Develop the ability to recognize and appreciate what you can do with all that you've been given and all that you've earned.

(20)

You can limit your development to avoid provoking insecurity in others, but it comes at the expense of all involved. You miss the opportunity to do your best; they miss the opportunity to think about doing more.

(21)

Insecurity usually stems from a desire to be seen in a certain way. If you can admit that you have this desire, you can admit that you have given too much of your power away. Develop true self-respect, and you'll be less affected by the negative opinion of others.

(22)

Yes, I'd prefer to be understood and, if possible, I'd prefer

notes:_____

_____

_____

to be appreciated. More than anything, I'd love to know that people find my work useful in some way. But if I'm not understood or appreciated, and if there's little evidence that others find my work useful, I'm going to do it anyway.

(23)

Time and effort are the currencies that will purchase your future. Regardless of what you want from life, invest them in a way that leads to growth. Set aside some of these "funds" for things that will help you become more.

(24)

Patience is medicine. Love is medicine. Gratitude is medicine. These states of mind can reduce or completely eliminate suffering.

(25)

By reducing the circuits reserved for craving, you make room for something better. By reducing the circuits reserved for judgement, you make room for something better. By reducing any self-destructive or counterproductive tendency, you clear the way for the establishment of something better within you.

(26)

Some reasonable goals: Do not bring more hatred into the

notes:_____

_____

_____

world, either by nurturing it in yourself or by intentionally provoking it in others. Do not bring more fear into the world, by nurturing it in yourself or provoking it in others. Insecurity, resentment, depression, lust; to the extent possible, do not intentionally bring more of these into the world.

(27)
What if we are driven by a desire to maintain our identity? And what if our identity isn't healthy? More specifically, what if we develop and nurture behaviors that lead to suffering because an unhealthy aspect of our identity compels us to do so? If that is the case, here's a much more powerful question: What happens to self-destructive impulses and behaviors when, with intentional effort, we *improve* our identity?

(28)
Every moment provides an opportunity to either correct what you've been doing wrong or build upon what you've been doing right. The past doesn't matter.

notes:_____

_____

_____

PERSONAL NOTES, EXPERIENCES, DREAMS, MEDITATIONS

(29)

I've changed so many things about the way I think, feel, and behave that I lean very heavily toward the idea that *all* of the programs that affect us negatively can be altered or completely replaced.

(30)

When I finally accepted (without resentment) that I *DO NOT* get to choose all outcomes, my suffering decreased significantly. Each day provides an opportunity to apply and benefit from this lesson, but on some days, it's needed more than others. Here's a simple example that anyone with a pet can probably relate to.

My 145-pound-dog Rocko (who I love with all my heart), has hurt himself a few times while playing. This last time was bad. He ran after his ball at full speed, apparently turned his front leg the wrong way, and immediately began limping. The way he was holding his leg looked really odd. I used to have major shoulder instability, and that's what it reminded me of—like a subluxation or possibly a dislocation.

Enter the truth: I don't get to choose if Rocko has a serious injury or not. I don't get to choose if he heals

notes:_____

_____

_____

to 100% within a couple weeks and never hurts himself again, or if his injury is so bad that it'll require some type of surgical intervention. All I can do is carefully assess the issue and choose a course of action. Stressing about the final outcome will produce *zero* value because I *do not* get to choose that part.

I wish I could have realized and embraced this concept decades ago, but I had to see it thousands of times in thousands of different ways before it finally clicked in my mind. It applies to so many things: I can't choose what people think. I can't choose how they behave. I can't choose what they believe or what they refuse to believe, what they approve of or what they ridicule. I don't get to choose how or when my loved ones will die or countless other things about my life that, if it were up to me, I'd likely change.

When I say that I "accept this without resentment," it simply means that I'm injecting some much-needed humility into my life experience. This universe isn't here to meet my expectations or satisfy my every wish. I can work to improve almost anything, but if some things remain outside of my control, I can only assume it's that way for a reason. One reason, if no other, is that it's helped me discover and develop an inner peace that transcends outward circumstances.

notes:_____

_____

_____

(31)

I can no longer tolerate those who demand sympathy for problems they create for themselves. I truly wish them well, but if they're unwilling to change, there is literally *nothing* I can do to help them.

(32)

I have no right or desire to make anyone believe anything. My objective is to simply share what I believe and why I believe it.

(33)

Regarding my mother (without judgement, without frustration): She has no inner drive to be well. In fact, there appears to be an overwhelming inner drive to be *unwell*, to intentionally harm herself physically and mentally. Is it self-hate? Is it an unconscious circuit seeking attention, assistance, reduced expectations? All of the above? Something else? I don't know, but it's very difficult to watch somebody you love slowly destroy themself.

(34)

Some neglect their physical and mental health so severely that it seems malicious.

(35)

You cannot help those who have no desire to help themselves.

notes:_____

_____

_____

(36)

Forgive them and see what happens to how you feel. Seriously, forgive them. Stop judging. They're not here to meet your expectations any more than you are here to meet theirs. They, like you, are here to live their life and learn their own lessons. By all means, protect yourself from harm, but don't waste your time and energy in judgement. You'll only bring additional suffering into the world.

HOW TO

(37)

You're tired of engaging in a certain thought process or behavior, so you commit to eliminating it. Things seem to be going well until, out of nowhere, you encounter a provocation that triggers the unwanted response. That's bad enough, but then your inner idiot (which caused the problem in the first place) tries to make things worse by offering you the opportunity to feel like a "failure." Don't take the bait.

Instead, simply accept that there are remaining pathways in your mind that need to be pruned, and new pathways that need to be created. Beating yourself up wastes energy that could be put to better use, and it invites the inner idiot to taunt you further. Listen closely. You'll realize it's simply protecting the thoughts and behaviors you're working to eliminate: "See,

notes:_____

_____

_____

you can't do it. You failed! Why bother trying? Just accept that this is who you are!" It doesn't know any better; ignore it.

(38)
Observe and assess the value of your reactions. It's the first step toward changing the way you habitually respond to the world. The next step is to understand that any reaction (healthy or unhealthy), can be made better or worse. If you doubt this, begin experimenting with that idea, and make sure to play the experiment out in *both* directions.

Assume you've observed an unhealthy reaction. Ask yourself: "OK, how could I have made that response significantly worse?" After you realize how far you could have gone in the wrong direction, ask yourself: "How could I have made my response significantly better?"

The purpose of this exercise is to develop an important concept: The initial unhealthy response is just one of an infinite number of responses that you can choose from. With some effort and patience, you'll realize that there isn't a single unhealthy response that you can't move into a healthier direction.

(39)
Lifelong improvement begins with observation. You need to consciously create an "observer" in your mind, a piece of your identity that monitors mental activity for destructive

notes:_____

_____

_____

thoughts and feelings. If you don't, you'll spend your life lost in the negative experiences that destructive thoughts and feelings create. But develop your ability to observe the mind, and everything changes. Now, the observer steps in on your behalf like a separate stream of consciousness; it interrupts the self-destructive process. It draws your attention to *what the mind is doing*. And because the observer exists *above* the destructive thoughts, feelings, and subsequent behaviors, it enables you to weaken and eliminate them over time.

(40)

I don't advocate ignoring reality; I advocate ignoring harmful responses to it.

GENERAL OBSERVATIONS

(41)

If it heals, it's medicine. If it only masks the symptoms, it's a drug.

(42)

Your *reaction* is what matters most, and that depends on the perspective you choose and the meaning you assign.

(43)

Everything we encounter affects us. Only we can decide how much and in what way.

notes:_____

_____

_____

(44)

At some point in your life, you will be offered the title of "victim." It's a trap. Reject the offer.

(45)

Avoid judging others. It benefits *you* more than them.

(46)

Just a handful of things moved me toward a much better life: self-awareness, gratitude, honesty, empathy, patience, and a desire to be of service to others.

(47)

Unfortunately, some people would rather die than confront and eliminate their self-destructive thoughts and behaviors.

(48)

Everything we do meets a need. If we have an unhealthy identity, we'll develop unhealthy habits to sustain it.

(49)

Self-destructive behaviors are driven by self-destructive impulses, and self-destructive impulses are driven by self-destructive, identity-based programs.

(50)

You can create a state within the body and mind that is

notes:_____

_____

_____

optimized for illness and deterioration, or you can create a state that is optimized for health and healing. The prescription for illness and deterioration is well known:

1. Regularly ingest things that cause harm to the body and mind.
2. Rarely ingest things the body and mind need to function properly.
3. Avoid regular movement and periodic exercise.
4. Embrace stressful thoughts and negative energy.

The prescription for health and healing is also well known:

1. Rarely ingest things that cause harm to the body and mind.
2. Regularly ingest things the body and mind need to function properly.
3. Embrace regular movement and periodic exercise.
4. Avoid stressful thoughts and negative energy.

notes:_____

_____

_____

SPIRITUAL

(51)

Forgive the deceiver and the deceived, but do not permit them to operate unchallenged.

(52)

Don't misunderstand the concept of "not judging" others. It doesn't mean ignore bad behavior. If your uncle Pete steals everything that isn't nailed down, asking him to watch your house while you're on vacation is probably a bad idea. Not judging isn't about ignoring reality; it's about acknowledging reality without feeding unhealthy ego and generating a bunch of ugly energy.

Example of *not* judging: "Pete steals—a lot. We can't trust him in the house. No way."

Example of judging: "Pete is a total scumbag; he'd steal his own mother's last dollar. I wouldn't loan that asshole a penny to save his life."

(53)

To the extent you can forgive the weakness in others, you overcome a weakness in yourself.

notes:_____

_____

_____

(54)

Conceit, hatred, fear, ingratitude, cruelty—when we invite them in, we poison ourselves and our world. Humility, forgiveness, courage, gratitude, empathy—when we invite them in, we do the opposite. We detoxify.

(55)

I can live my life in a state of mind that's healthy and grateful (then die), or I can live my life in a state that's unhealthy and ungrateful (then die). I choose the former. I'm not saying it's easy, but it's superior to the alternative.

(56)

I'm sure it helps that I believe consciousness survives physical death. Physical death and suffering are a lot easier to deal with when you see them as fleeting moments in an ageless cycle of birth, death, and spiritual evolution.

(57)

When I was young, it hurt me deeply when others said or believed things about me that were untrue. Many years later, there are two things that bring me complete peace: (1) the fact that I know the truth and (2) my belief that, when they die, they will know too.

notes:_____

_____

_____

(58)

You are not your body. You are a piece of the ageless intelligence that created and occupies it.

(59)

Bodies are lost; life is not.

(60)

The memories of those we've lost can fill us for the rest of our lives with limitless love and gratitude, or they can fill us with limitless suffering. It depends on the following: Do we focus on the riches they added to our life, or do we focus only on a desire for them to contribute more?

notes:_____

_____

_____

CHAPTER 5

Circuits

(1)
Habits of thought exist as biological structures in your brain. Unfortunately, some of these biological structures impede your ability. Assume, with effort, that you can reshape these impediments into something else. You can turn them into new biological structures that *increase* your ability—so much so that the formerly "impossible" becomes automatic, effortless.

(2)
When a circuit produces harmful desires, the circuit itself is harmful. Limited to the perspective that created it, the harmful circuit will *always* entice you with exaggerated visions of "reward." It doesn't know how to do anything else. It isn't capable of presenting an accurate corresponding vision of *costs*, because that perspective was never included in its original structure. It's designed to press the *desire* button in your nervous system, nothing more. You can't expect it to calculate accurately.

notes:_____

_____

_____

When you thoughtlessly embrace the desire and chase the miscalculated reward, the circuit becomes stronger. However, if you honestly scrutinize the reward long enough, the miscalculation becomes more obvious. The desire, and the circuit, become weaker.

Regardless of what you choose, never forget that "you" are not the circuits that create desire (healthy or otherwise). *You* are the one who decides whether to embrace and strengthen them or reject and weaken them. You are the one who decides whether or not to calculate accurately.

(3)

If you currently earn an average middle-class salary, and I offer you a job that pays $8,000 per day, there's a good chance you'll be interested. But if I explain later that the job requires special equipment, and that you must rent the equipment from me at a cost of $18,000 per day, you'd quickly realize I wasn't offering you anything of value. In fact, you'd be insulted. (Worse than asking you to work for free, I'm asking you to pay me an extra $10,000 when the workday is over.)

This touches on the importance of accurately calculating rewards and costs. It's painfully obvious in an example like the one I've just given, but it's much more difficult when it comes to calculating the value of bad habits. That's because

notes:_____

_____

_____

bad habits pay their greatest rewards in the beginning. They offer an immediate, short-lived benefit. However, bad habits come with inescapable costs. The costs are small at first, but they're not short lived; they accumulate and compound over time. Before long, the persistent and growing costs dwarf any value derived from the fleeting reward. But by then, our behavior is completely automated. It requires a conscious effort to recalculate before we can see the obvious truth: The habit has generated a loss. If we maintain the habit, the loss will only grow.

(4)

As you redirect energy into a newly created mental circuit, the paths leading to it grow wider; the circuit becomes stronger. Before long, your mind will access it effortlessly. Meanwhile, old circuits that you've been diverting energy away from will begin to weaken; their pathways will be "pruned" and disappear. The formerly connected neurons in the unwanted circuit will now be free to engage in more productive activity.

(5)

Identify and decommission the machinery that produces poison within you. Identify and decommission the structures in your mind that impede your progress. How? By no longer employing them and by creating new structures to take their place.

notes:_____

_____

_____

(6)

In the simplest terms, it's about rewiring your default reaction; that's it. If you're lucky, it will happen in a flash of deep insight, and no other effort will be necessary, but don't count on that. It often requires many repetitions to build or replace the circuits in your mind.

(7)

As you weaken the unhealthy circuits in your mind, their enticements become less convincing. You finally see them for what they are: nothing more than an invitation to suffer.

(8)

Self-directed rewiring boils down to identifying counterproductive circuits and consciously directing your nervous system to "disconnect" them. Once the connections are pruned, your brain can put those neurons to more productive use.

(9)

Establish powerful primary circuits in your brain, circuits that are built on healthy principles. This will create a conflict whenever unhealthy circuits attempt to take root or sway your thinking in the wrong direction.

(10)

This isn't about avoiding reality; it's about altering the way

notes:_____

_____

_____

you habitually react to life. It's about choosing whether or not you'll continue "adding harm" unnecessarily; whether you'll find ways to develop strength under difficult circumstances, or use circumstances as an excuse to engage in self-destructive thinking and behavior.

(11)
Your mental activity literally shapes the physical connections in your brain. When your brain changes, *you* change. It's your job to decide which type of change you want. (Change for better or change for worse?)

(12)
The role of the "observer" is to notice negative reactions within the body. When the observer notices negative energy, you can then trace the energy back to its source (the inner narrative or mental image that prompted it). This is how you discover, and begin the process of eliminating, unhealthy circuits in your mind.

HOW TO

(13)
Self-destructive habits are driven by positive associations. If you'd like to create the desire to *abstain*, you need to get honest. You need to create *negative* associations that more accurately reflect the destructive reality of the habit. When

notes:_____

_____

_____

your negative associations become dominant, abstinence requires no special effort. It becomes as natural as abstaining from anything else that you find unappealing.

(14)
When you observe an unwanted response, label the circuit that created it. "That's the circuit that always wants me to worry. ...That's the circuit that wants me to be a slave to 'X'. ...That's the circuit that wants me to be outraged. ...That's the circuit that wants me to feel bad about myself."

How do you know the circuit *wants* to produce these states of being? Because the narrative it presents can *only* lead to that state. The circuit frames things in a way that can only generate a negative response; that's its job. If we assume that you're the manager of your mind, can you guess what your job is?

(15)
Just because your automatic mind offers a programmed response doesn't mean you have to accept it. Why not practice rejecting some offers here and there? Start with little things, negotiate a bit, and see how much you can improve responses that aren't very useful.

(16)
Negative emotions are almost always traceable to a negative

notes:_____

_____

_____

inner narrative. (Your inner voice says something that you identify with, and your nervous system reacts accordingly.) For instance, if you feel like somebody is taking advantage of you, it's reasonable to assume that your mind will create a negative narrative about the situation. Maybe something like: "She's crazy if she thinks I am going to keep driving her all over town. I'm not her personal taxi service!" Or maybe your mind is complaining about some other issue: "I am never going to get this done. It's taking forever!"

When you hear an inner narrative like this, pause for a moment. *Think* about the words. If you're using the phrase "I am" in your statements, it indicates that you are fully identified with the statements and, by extension, fully identified with the negative response. But why would you choose to identify with either of these? Does it make sense? Not if you believe that "you" are more than the spontaneous narratives and reactions that erupt in your brain.

As discussed elsewhere in this book, most of our mental activity is driven by previously established mental programs. These programs automate our response to as many things as they can. If the programs are healthy, they will produce healthy narratives and emotions. But if the programs are unhealthy—if they specialize in generating anger, impatience, pessimism, or other destructive energies—they will generate *negative* narratives and emotions. Identifying

notes:_____

_____

_____

with the healthy ones makes sense, but identifying with the unhealthy ones, not so much.

If you can accept that premise, it'll enable you to notice problems and make changes when necessary. You'll be able to create some distance between "you" (the observer) and the unthinking reaction by simply asking yourself, "**Where did that come from**?" Don't be surprised if you hear an insightful reply, *especially* if you've accepted the idea of unhealthy programs waiting around for a chance to do their job. "That's the program that loves to fill me with outrage," or, "That's the program that can't wait to generate pessimism and make me feel bad about myself."

Again, *pausing* to consider the words and/or asking, "Where did that come from?" creates some distance between *you* and the unthinking knee-jerk narrative that you were originally offered. In that space, you'll realize that the first narrative is just one of an infinite number that you could choose from. If you want a more disturbing narrative that creates even more negative energy, you could easily whip one up. Or, if you'd prefer a less disturbing narrative, that's an option too—something like, "She's not going to be happy, but we're gonna have to talk about this." Or, "This is going to take longer than I thought. I've just got to calm down and be patient."

notes:_____

_____

_____

GENERAL REMINDERS AND OBSERVATIONS

(17)

In one way or another, we can improve ourselves until the day we die.

(18)

Unhealthy ego will say, "This is a good reason to be angry!" But is there ever a *good* reason to *be* angry? Unhealthy ego will justify itself. It will say, "This is a normal reaction!" But does that mean it's a superior choice? When dealing with unhealthy ego, remember that it's *your* responsibility to soften or reject its narratives.

(19)

Do, *observe*, and then determine the next step. This is the most peaceful way to get anything done.

(20)

Focus on things you *can* control; you'll make progress and feel empowered. Focus on things you *can't* control; you'll make yourself sick and feel helpless.

(21)

It's not uncommon for people to seek relief in activities that, ironically, lead them to greater suffering.

notes:_____

_____

_____

(22)
The more you feed an unhealthy desire, the more that desire feeds on you.

(23)
Think of sin as *error*. Not in the sense that you'll suffer in hell for committing it, but in the sense that error creates suffering *here and now*. Not as a punishment, but in accordance with immutable laws of cause and effect.

(24)
Tearing others down creates the illusion of building yourself up, but the illusion doesn't last, and unlike actually improving yourself, the illusion cannot make you stronger.

(25)
Any good coach, teacher, or mentor will tell their student where they're weak. They point out inadequacies in order to help the other person become stronger. That is completely different than deriving joy from belittling people. If a person enjoys tearing others down, that feeds something unhealthy within them. It doesn't lead anywhere good.

(26)
Ordinary people look for faults in others. Extraordinary people find and fix the faults within themselves. Don't be ordinary. Your life, and the world, will be better for it.

notes:_____

_____

_____

(27)

When you provide hatred a place to express itself, it enters the world through you. When you provide insecurity a place to express itself, it enters the world through you. Fear, resentment, depression, lust—these harmful energies need a body to enter this world, and by providing that body (or by intentionally provoking these energies in others), we diminish ourselves and the world in the process.

(28)

How do people become blind to an obvious truth? What is the mental mechanism that impedes their ability to see? Answer: Rather than observe evidence with honest eyes, they begin sorting every observation according to its ability to confirm what they've already concluded. Evidence that supports their conclusions is eagerly accepted, while evidence that contradicts their conclusions (no matter how compelling) is rejected.

(29)

When unhealthy ego is sufficiently involved, ignoring facts becomes an act of self-preservation.

(30)

Even if it comes with great personal and professional costs, even if it proves them wrong, those who prioritize TRUTH are driven to find it. You'll notice the opposite in those who

notes:_____

_____

_____

prioritize POWER. Truth is whatever they want it to be; whatever convinces you to believe and obey.

(31)
The brain, like other physical parts of the human body, is shaped by what it's fed and how it's used.

(32)
Results provide the most convincing argument.

(33)
Persistence, like water, can erode the most durable barriers over time.

(34)
Success in life depends less on what you encounter and more on how you respond to it.

(35)
Some people have no desire to help themselves. If you jump in to save them, they'll only drag you down with them.

(36)
Express gratitude for what you have rather than resentment for what you don't.

notes:_____

_____

_____

(37)

If rejection can be used as a weapon, so too can acceptance. Defend yourself.

(38)

Don't embrace impulses that you cannot, in good conscience, act on.

(39)

It's foolish to establish an irritated response to something that's *guaranteed* to happen over and over again.

(40)

Appreciate recognition but know better than to crave it.

(41)

Strip away the mental errors and fill that space with something better.

(42)

Beware of the mongers (fear, hate, and resentment).

(43)

Don't mistake the programming for the programmer. You are the latter.

notes:_____

_____

_____

(44)

As long as you learn from your mistakes, then what you've done was not a waste.

(45)

No matter who you are, no matter what you do, somebody (somewhere) will judge you negatively. Knowing this, it makes no sense to assign undue significance to the opinions of others.

(46)

You can't stop somebody from suffering the consequences of bad choices. You can offer help or advice, but the *solution* to their troubles is ultimately up to them. You can't do their work for them.

(47)

When you find yourself in an unwanted program/response, that is your greatest opportunity. Anything you do to prevent the program from running at full force will weaken it. From simply noticing and refusing to embrace it, to stopping it dead in its tracks with a firm redirect, *disruption* engages the rewiring process.

(48)

Status-dependent individuals tend to feel threatened when somebody steals their spotlight. It makes them feel inferior

notes:_____

_____

_____

or diminished in some way. The truth, of course, is that they are not diminished; they are the same as they were five minutes prior to the encounter. It's only their ego's opinion of itself that has been momentarily downsized.

(49)
Note to self: There will always be unreasonable people. If you can't come to terms with that, you might just be one of them.

SPECIFICALLY ON FEAR, GUILT/REGRET, AND SELFISHNESS

(50)
It's been said that "there is no courage without fear." This is untrue. If you know that you face danger, but you choose to move forward anyway, then you've demonstrated courage. Fear is unnecessary. It drains energy that can be put to more productive use.

(51)
You don't need fear to understand risks and to adjust your behavior accordingly.

(52)
I know that if I jump naked off the Grand Canyon Skywalk, the odds of survival are practically zero. It doesn't require "fear of death" to prevent me from giving it a try. The mere

notes:_____

_____

_____

fact that I prefer "more life" to certain death is enough to inform my decision.

(53)
We ought to be aware of risk and plan accordingly; that's the best anyone can do. Adding fear adds nothing of value.

(54)
Practically none of our fears come to pass, and of those that might, it will take more than fear for us to stop them.

(55)
Everything that you can do in a state of fear you can do in a state of heightened awareness. You can be aware of danger without fearing it.

(56)
In the absence of morality, fear can be useful. For instance, fear of getting caught might prevent you from stealing. In the absence of discernment, fear can be useful. It might prevent you from jumping into a cage with a lion. But morality and discernment should both come with maturity. So, perhaps it would be more accurate to say, "In the absence of maturity, fear can be useful."

(57)
Unhealthy ego is self-limiting at best, self-destructive at

notes:_____

_____

_____

worst. As you begin to escape its influence, it'll try to regain control any way it can. One of its favorite tactics is to lure you back with guilt and regret. Don't fall for it. If an unpleasant past memory pops into your head, acknowledge the mistake, sincerely apologize in your heart to anyone you might have hurt, and move on. Don't use the past as an excuse to engage in self-hate or ridicule. It benefits no one.

(58)

When the inner idiot wants you to hate yourself for coming up short or making a mistake, don't hesitate to ask it some questions. "How long should I regret this? How long should I hate myself? Is 10 minutes long enough? 10 hours? 10 days? 10 years? What is the benefit? Will it change anything? Will it make me a better person, or will it simply waste time and energy that I could use to improve who I am and what I contribute?"

(59)

Feeling guilty today about errors corrected long ago is a waste of time and energy. It's much better to invest that time and energy into identifying and correcting the errors that remain.

(60)

I won't punish myself today for mistakes I made in the past because the person who made those mistakes is long dead. The moment I became strong enough, I killed him.

notes:_____

_____

_____

(61)

Nobody can change the mistakes in their past, but anyone can change the thinking that led to them. If you've righted your mind, you've righted the source of your wrongs. You've issued the most meaningful and enduring apology possible.

(62)

All human behavior is ultimately selfish because it seeks to satisfy prioritized desires. However, there's a difference between ethical and unethical selfishness. Ethical selfishness seeks an informed/voluntary exchange of value. There's no willingness to mislead, coerce, or cause harm in pursuit of desire. Unethical selfishness is the opposite. It contributes value only by accident, and it embraces deception, coercion, and even the harm of others.

(63)

Deriving pleasure from helping others is an example of ethical selfishness. Deriving pleasure from harming others is an example of unethical selfishness. In both cases, the person is motivated by their own self-interest (pursuit of pleasure), but one achieves their desire in a way that's mutually beneficial, and the other achieves their desire at the direct expense of somebody else.

notes:

PERSONAL NOTES, EXPERIENCES, DREAMS, MEDITATIONS

(64)

When it comes to effortless abstinence from self-destructive thoughts, impulses, and behavior or effortless fidelity to constructive thoughts, impulses, and behaviors, I know from personal experience that *both* are inevitable when you successfully rewire the circuits in your mind.

(65)

Today, in a state of calm awareness, I revisited a familiar thought regarding self-destructive people: "It's sad that they suffer unnecessarily." Instantly, awareness corrected me: "Most of their suffering is not unnecessary. It is tied to the choices they have made and continue to make. Their suffering is only unnecessary in the sense that they can choose, and could have chosen, differently."

(66)

February 16th, 2016: One of the most comforting meditations I've had in a long time. "If you truly believe in your heart that you're doing what you're supposed to do, you can focus on your work with peace and conviction. You can do the work without the nagging distractions of 'what if this?' or 'what about that?' It doesn't mean that you don't want the work to be appreciated. It doesn't mean that you don't want

notes:_____

_____

_____

to ease the stress of your current financial position or even regain access to things that you've lost the ability to afford. It simply means that you need to get the work done, and, once you have (regardless of outcome), you will *know* that you've spent your time in the best way possible. *The work* provides the greatest reward."

(67)
Note to self: I believe I'm here to choose between two paths: one that leads to the liberation of myself and others, or one that leads to enslavement. That's it. I've made my choice, and I will live accordingly.

(68)
It's not that I don't sometimes feel pain, anger, stress, or any other negative emotions; it's that I refuse to nurture them. I don't embrace them and feed them energy. Instead, I observe them, acknowledge them, and then state the obvious: I can do better than that. If I choose the opposite response, I'm essentially "practicing" and strengthening those negative emotions. I'm wiring them deeper into my nervous system, making it easier to slip into them again in the future.

(69)
As I've strengthened my "observer," I've noticed many programs running in the background of my mind that make no sense at all. Today, for the first time ever, I realized I've got

notes:_____

_____

_____

a program that creates unjustifiable tension whenever I have to drive to an unfamiliar address. I mean, today's road trip couldn't have been any simpler to map out and follow, yet this "unfamiliar-destination" program jumped into action anyway. The background stress level might have been appropriate if there was a chance that I could drive 50 miles off course, be hours late, *AND* have no way of contacting the person waiting for me to pick them up. But there was no way that could happen. I literally only had to drive 10 minutes down the street and take a left on a road that I was pretty sure I knew the location of.

Again, as I've continued strengthening the *observer*, its ability to notice caustic background energy/programs has improved a lot. I probably created that negative "driving circuit" the first time I got lost looking for an address 35 years ago, and it's been there (just beneath my conscious awareness) ever since.

Today, when the observer noticed the tension and calmly asked, "What the hell is that all about?" my conscious/rational mind looked at it and immediately identified how ridiculous it was. It then proceeded to offer an alternate/sane representation of the situation: "First of all, you're probably not going to miss the turn. Second, even if you do, you *might* be five minutes late. Is it really that bad?" Instantly the irrational tension disappeared, and, best I can tell, it took the program that created the tension along with it.

notes:_____

_____

_____

(70)

Everything provides an opportunity to strengthen yourself in some way. Using another one of my crazy dreams as an example, last night I dreamt that lava was moving beneath asphalt in a parking lot. I was showing it to Teri (my wife) when the ground suddenly shifted between us and opened up. It threw me forward, and a wave of thick asphalt immediately folded over me. I was entombed. I knew I was done, and all I could say is "Oh shit, SHIT!" because Teri had seen the whole thing, and she couldn't do anything to help me. I knew how panicked she had to be and how bad it would ultimately hurt her. Then I woke up.

Rather than dwell on the psychological pain I felt in the dream, I processed the experience like this: "Yes, you can unexpectedly die in an instant; things like that can happen. Nobody wants it, but if it happens, it's just something we've got to be prepared for and deal with. Consider that dream your reminder to be grateful for every single day."

Expanding on that just a bit, I regularly experience *very* disturbing things in my dreams. When I was younger, they'd bother me long after I woke up. Then, I learned to look at the dreams differently. I learned to look at them as an opportunity to "live through" something very disturbing, without *actually* having to live through it in real life. I learned to see the dreams as an opportunity to develop useful insights and strength that I could apply in the real world.

notes:_____

_____

_____

CHAPTER 6

Fitness

(1)

An *easy* exercise routine that you enjoy doing is infinitely better than a hard exercise routine that you hate. The reason is simple: The routine you enjoy will get you off your butt for a lifetime, while the one you hate is unlikely to last more than a few months.

(2)

Exercise strengthens both the body *and* the mind. It activates the good genes and downregulates the bad. For most of us, exercise provides the surest path to greater health, happiness, and longevity.

(3)

When most people decide to get fit, they make the mistake of pushing themselves way too hard. It's unfortunate, but understandable. The enormous value and relative ease of establishing *general* fitness is rarely spoken of these days. Instead, fitness culture only seems to recognize the value of achieving specialized or competitive-level fitness. Again,

notes:_____

_____

_____

this is a shame because the majority of health and quality-of-life benefits occur when a person moves from being "unfit" to just plain "fit."

No, the average fit person won't be running a five-minute mile or deadlifting 700 pounds; that requires specialized/competitive-level fitness. Instead, they'll be more like a healthy 18-year-old. They'll possess good general mobility. If they want, they'll be able to run a mile in 10 or 12 minutes without feeling like they're going to die. They'll be able to deadlift or squat most or all of their bodyweight without hurting themselves. Their body composition will stop moving in the wrong direction and begin moving in the right direction. And if all that's not enough, the positive effects on their mood, hormones, immune system, energy levels, metabolism, mental clarity, and general health will provide the *greatest benefits* of all.

People who establish an enjoyable exercise routine, a routine they actually look forward to, instinctively stop worrying about how many calories they're burning. They're too busy focusing on (and experiencing) the cascade of mental and physical health benefits that exercise creates, benefits that build and persist long after a 20- or 30-minute session ends. And here's the best part of all: It's possible to establish and maintain general fitness into our 80s and beyond with a tiny fraction of the effort that specialized/competitive-level fitness requires.

notes:_____

_____

_____

(4)

The young tend to view exercise as a path to social and sexual status. (That's where I started.) Hopefully, as they age, they'll realize that there are more rewarding primary objectives to aim for. The drive can shift to something healthier, like physical, mental, and even spiritual health. Each of these provide major benefits, and the social and sexual benefits of being fit and healthy (if the mind is still concerned with such things) will still be there.

(5)

Super-human feats of strength and ability are impressive, but they're *not necessary* for living an extraordinary, physically unrestricted life. For this, general fitness is all we need. People in their 80s have managed to achieve it, and people in their 100s have managed to maintain it. So, if you haven't already, why not add taking care of yourself to the list of things you enjoy doing?

(6)

Is there such a thing as spiritually motivated fitness? Yes, I think so. I would define it this way: not driven by a desire to gain power over others (via your physical appeal or physical ability) and not driven by a desire to be seen as superior to others. Instead, spiritually motivated fitness is guided by a deep appreciation and respect for your body and mind. As levels of development are achieved, the psychological

notes:_____

_____

_____

reward is a profound and sometimes overwhelming sense of gratitude for the amount of progress that's possible.

(7)

A common goal of exercise is to improve ourselves physically, maybe lose some fat, gain some muscle and endurance. But we can use exercise to improve ourselves in more powerful ways. We can turn workouts into a form of physical meditation. It only requires that we shift our focus a bit during exercise toward building mental clarity, or tearing down useless thoughts, or strengthening our capacity for gratitude and spiritual health. The new *gains* are awesome, and you'll still acquire the others (less fat, more muscle, better endurance) in the process.

(8)

Fitness gratitude versus vanity:

A person looks in the mirror, realizes their exercise has paid off, and they feel a deep sense of gratitude for what they've been able to accomplish. Another person looks in the mirror, realizes their exercise has paid off, and they feel a sense of power and superiority over others. The former has set his or herself up for a lifetime of rewards. The latter has set his or herself up for suffering. (When confronted with anyone who looks better, they will feel uncomfortable. That feeling will intensify as the decades pass and the mirror becomes less kind.)

notes:_____

_____

_____

(9)

What is "never-enough fitness"? Imagine the following: Bob is a healthy, adventurous 21-year-old man when his boat sinks off the coast of a deserted island. He's able to swim to safety, and the island has plenty of fresh water, but there isn't any food. When rescuers finally locate Bob, two months have passed and he is clinging to life, severely malnourished, little more than skin and bones. If you were in charge of nursing Bob back to health, which of the following two prescriptions would you choose?

RX 1: Give Bob the nutrition he needs to restore his body weight and his former excellent health.

RX 2: Same as prescription 1 except for the following: Once Bob has fully regained his weight and his health, tell him that he must never stop gaining weight. Explain that if he isn't gaining weight, he's moving in the wrong direction (back toward starvation and malnutrition). Make sure he understands that no matter how many pounds he packs on, he must strive to continue gaining, forever.

Can we agree that Bob does not need to follow prescription 2 in order to recover and maintain the good health he formerly enjoyed? If so, let's substitute Bob's "compromised health caused by lack of food" for something way more common in today's society: compromised health caused by lack of exercise.

notes:_____

_____

_____

Suddenly we realize that many exercise experts promote something very similar to prescription 2. That is, no matter how much progress you make it's never enough. You must push harder today so you can push harder tomorrow, so you can push harder next month and the month after—forever. The idea of simply reaching a *healthy* level of fitness (unspecialized/not competitive) and then *maintaining* that level of fitness is nowhere to be found.

Granted, if somebody competes professionally or their livelihood depends on 10-plus hours of weekly exercise, then the never-enough mindset makes sense. Or, if somebody has simply decided they want to swim 25 miles, run 100 miles, bike 400 miles, or deadlift a car "because they can," that's fine too. But these are people who've chosen to be specialists, and, like any specialist, their life will largely revolve around the thing they specialize in. They're definitely experts, but they're not where beginners should go for advice.

Beginners will do much better with a *slow and comfortable* introduction to exercise. Just enough to get the blood flowing and the mood elevated. Just enough to make them look forward to the next scheduled workout. This is how they'll determine which type of exercise they like. This is how they'll develop the habit and desire. From there, they can ramp things up to whatever level of intensity and fitness that fits their goals.

notes:_____

_____

_____

(10)

Crappy food, crappy drinks, crappy *thoughts*, and crappy habits accelerate biological aging. Healthy food, healthy drinks, healthy thoughts and habits reverse and/or slow biological aging. So, here's the question: Would you rather experience the age-related damage of an unhealthy 70-year-old when you're 50, or would you prefer to express the vitality of a healthy 50-year-old when you're 70? And if you're already biologically older than your chronological age, would you rather be biologically *younger and healthier* five years from now? If you're breathing and willing to improve, it's not too late.

(11)

What level of strength, mobility, balance, and energy are required to live a normal, unrestricted life? A healthy, untrained 18-year-old provides a good model. They can work, play, and socialize without limits. They have the energy and ability to walk their dog, ride their bike, or go skiing. They can dance if they want to dance, go for a hike, or a stroll on the beach. They don't dread walking up or down stairs, let alone walking across a parking lot or simply getting out of a chair. That level of 18-year-old general fitness can be maintained into your 70s, 80s, 90s, and beyond (see George Jedenoff). Why not add those decades to your quality-of-life span?

notes:_____

_____

_____

(12)
I've optimized diet, exercise, and lifestyle to avoid using doctors and drugs. I've seen what happens when people choose the opposite approach (when they use doctors and drugs to avoid addressing their diet, exercise, and lifestyle). I've yet to see the latter approach end well.

(13)
View your body as a *very* generous friend that has provided you a place to live.

GENERAL REMINDERS AND OBSERVATIONS

(14)
Reject the obvious lie that confidence is derived from the praise of others. To the greatest extent possible, prevent yourself from *needing* them to approve of your beliefs and behavior. Instead, consult your conscience. Develop intellectually honest standards, and work faithfully to achieve and improve them. This inevitably leads to something far greater than external approval, the courage of your convictions.

(15)
People who want to think less of you will find and accept any reason to do so. Let them. Unless you've openly wished or done them harm, the problem isn't with you.

notes:_____

_____

_____

(16)

If you've spent years identifying with a particular reaction, you might not notice the triggered state of mind until after it has run its course. That's why, to get better at reprogramming, it's necessary to pay closer attention to your thoughts, emotions, and impulses. By doing this, you'll get progressively better at *observing/noticing* when an unwanted program has been activated. That's step one.

Step two can also be challenging at first. The moment you detect an undesirable reaction, create distance between YOU (the conscious observer) and the program that's creating the unwanted narrative and reaction. One easy way to create this distance is to simply *reply* to the programmed response the same way you'd reply to a separate person. You might say: "I've been responding that way for a long time now, and I'm tired of it. I'm looking for better options." Or, maybe a more direct, less-polite reply is more your speed (use your imagination). Regardless of the reply you choose, it prevents you from fully embracing and identifying with the program. As you get better at seeing and disrupting it, you'll get better at cutting the flow of energy it needs to survive.

(17)

If nothing else, acknowledging a weakness helps to keep it in check. It creates a conflict, an inner awareness that "I *should* choose differently," or at least "I *should* exercise some

notes:_____

_____

_____

restraint." However, sometimes people choose to embrace one of their weaknesses. They justify it. They exaggerate its value and ignore or minimize its costs. They incorporate it into part of their accepted identity. From that point forward, the weakness can only grow. And as it grows, its capacity to cause harm (emotionally, physically, financially, spiritually) grows with it.

(18)
You can easily have diametrically opposed circuits within the same brain. Once you realize this, the absurdity of identifying with unhealthy circuits becomes clear. Also, the solution reveals itself: Strengthen the circuits you want; weaken and eliminate the ones that you don't.

(19)
Overbearing, dismissive, and condescending. These are traits of unhealthy people who are only interested in proving that they're right and you're wrong, regardless of whether or not it's true. They have a right to be this way. You have a right to not waste your time arguing with them.

(20)
Never give something too much power over you. If you notice that you already have, challenge the exaggerated significance you've assigned, and begin taking your power back.

notes:_____

_____

_____

(21)

Why would you want to forgive a person who lied about you, betrayed you, ripped you off, or worse? Answer: to protect yourself from additional harm. If that answer doesn't make sense, it's because you haven't yet realized the cost of harboring and continually producing stressful/negative energy. You haven't calculated the cost of keeping that ugliness alive in your head. In this context, forgiveness doesn't mean "pretend nothing happened" or "pretend what they did is OK." Rather, it means "I'm not going to use what happened as an excuse to poison myself with negative energy; I'm not giving them that level of power over me." Sure, it's easier said than done, but it's worth the effort. Find a way.

(22)

Sometimes you'll consciously observe: "My mind is offering negative narratives that can only lead to an unhealthy response." That's good. You'll probably avoid an unwanted reaction. Other times, you might realize that you've already slipped into an unhealthy response. In that case, you can probably minimize the intensity and duration of the episode. In the worst-case scenario, you'll be so taken in that you won't even realize what has happened until *after* the negative state has passed. In that case, the only thing to do is acknowledge that it happened, figure out how to make it less likely in the future, and avoid adding harm by beating yourself up for being human.

notes:_____

_____

_____

(23)

Ego/identity emerges from the acquired circuits in your mind, circuits that automatically respond without conscious thought. To the extent the circuits are healthy, they'll give rise to things like gratitude, patience, humility, honesty, and self-control. To the extent they're unhealthy, they'll give rise to ingratitude, impatience, arrogance, dishonesty, and craving. For better or worse, each circuit affects the ongoing development of your ego/identity. Without conscious intervention, the stronger circuits will govern trajectory.

(24)

It's easy to recognize a weed in the garden as something that needs "pulled," but a mental weed can manipulate you into thinking it's your friend. It can manipulate you into thinking it's who you are. When a mental weed hijacks your consciousness, you see the world through its eyes. You feel what it feels; you want what it wants. You don't realize that it's nothing but a giant weed that took root in the garden of your mind. It only survives and grows because you haven't pulled it, and because you continue to feed it.

(25)

An email exchange with a friend:

He wrote: "Think positive thoughts about yourself. Nice advice. But that's not a valid psychological theory."

notes:_____

_____

_____

My reply: "Sure, but 'think negative thoughts about yourself' isn't terribly valid either."

He wrote: "I know three people with low self-esteem. Each of them is tremendously caring, hard-working people… One of them is a genius, and his academic prowess is hard to deny. He still disparages himself in other ways. And all three of them have trouble setting boundaries where others can harm them. The opposite anecdote is that criminal sociopaths (such as serial killers) seem to have lots of self-esteem. Gang members seem to get increased self-esteem from belonging to the gang."

My reply: "Sounds like you're saying, 'People who have a low opinion of themselves tend to be better humans than people who have a high opinion of themselves.' This touches on the healthy versus unhealthy ego stuff that I started to talk about when we were playing pool. If I feel good about myself because I've destroyed a self-destructive impulse to ingest alcohol, it's not the same as if I feel good about myself because I'm good at conning old people out of their life's savings. You can feel good about yourself for *good* reasons, or you can feel good about yourself for bad reasons. (It's not that high self-esteem is inherently good or bad.) However, I do believe that those who choose *bad* reasons to feel good about themselves (conning/harming others) only secure superficial and fleeting 'confidence.' A far cry from the real thing.

notes:_____

_____

_____

"It's worth noting that this works both ways. You can feel bad about yourself for good or for bad reasons too. As an example, when I was a liar, druggy, and thief (10 years old to 15 years old), I felt bad about myself for a good reason. The pain was justified, and it eventually led to improvements in how I thought and behaved. My reward for making the improvements was greater self-esteem. And why not? I believe that's a natural and healthy process. Notice that the source of self-esteem has nothing to do with how I compare to other people, nor does it have anything to do with me seeking power over other people. Rather, it's based entirely on gaining power over myself and improving how I compared to my former self. I'd improved, in an area within my control, *in line with my conscience.*"

(26)
When you soften your judgement of others (when you stop poisoning yourself with self-righteous, hateful energy), it benefits you more than them.

POLITICS

(27)
Hypnotic susceptibility varies from person to person, but people who are easily hypnotized share a common characteristic: They are *willing* to surrender control of their mind to the hypnotist. As a result, they're far more likely to

notes:_____

_____

_____

do what they're told. If the hypnotist says, "When I click my fingers, you'll be a duck," it won't be long before you see them waddling around on the floor, quacking like a duck and flapping their non-existent wings.

Not surprisingly, those who are unwilling to surrender control of their mind are nearly impossible to hypnotize. They consciously resist the process of hypnosis and, as a result, they won't be triggered by the hypnotist's commands. Makes sense, right? If you're willing to be hypnotized, you're more easily triggered and controlled. If you're unwilling to be hypnotized, you can't be triggered and controlled. But what happens if you consent to being hypnotized without knowing it?

If we remove the obvious "hypnotist" from the equation, things get a little more disturbing because we're still left with the concepts of being triggered and controlled by other people. In this case, we'll swap a hypnotist that's barking commands for the media and its social-engineering experts. Instead of saying, "You will be a duck," they say, "When we want you to be terrified, you will be terrified. When we want you to be outraged, you will be outraged. When we want you to feel superior or judgmental, you will obey!" To the extent we're unaware of hypnotists using media to trigger and control us, we run the risk of unknowingly surrendering our minds to their hypnosis.

notes:_____

_____

_____

(28)

Propaganda is created to produce a hypnotic/suggestable state of mind. Its purpose is to evoke predictable emotions and a *desire* to obey the will of those who wrote the script. Easily falsifiable narratives and irrational/useless procedures are valuable in that they test the depth of hypnosis and obedience. It is, quite literally, a form of mind control.

(29)

School taught the rules: An authority provides the answer, the child repeats it, and that makes the child "right." Sadly, many carry this programming into adulthood. They don't want to *think*; they want to be told. Instead of questioning authority, they sneer at those who do.

(30)

Many politicians and bureaucrats hide their lust for power behind compassionate narratives. They are excellent at fooling well-meaning people. Therefore, it's best to completely ignore the benevolent ends that they claim to pursue. Focus instead on the methods they propose. And when their methods are so poor that they require blind trust and obedience—so poor that scrutiny must be censored and punished—let there be no doubt as to what they're really after.

notes:_____

_____

_____

(31)

They were trained and credentialed by the system. They depend on the system for their reputation, income, and retirement. Many have worked decades to squeeze their way into very thin cracks of opportunity and prestige. When they inevitably see the corruption, they have a choice: They can "do what's right" and lose everything, or they can look the other way. They can be smeared, humiliated, and banished from the ivory tower forever, or they can parrot the official narrative and prove their loyalty. Very few will find the courage to honestly question (let alone denounce) the "consensus" that emerges under these circumstances. And that's exactly why the system is dangerous and why nobody should thoughtlessly defer to the "experts" who are put forward to represent it.

(32)

The liars want censorship because it prevents their lies from being exposed, and the believers want censorship because it prevents their beliefs from being challenged.

(33)

Divide people into groups. Make them fear and hate the other side *so* much that they become psychologically incapable of honestly critiquing the actions of their own group's leaders. That's the trick. From that point forward, right and wrong becomes a matter of "who did it" instead of what was done.

notes:_____

_____

_____

Team A will ignore the transgressions of Team A; Team B will ignore the transgressions of Team B, and the ruling class (playing one team off the other) will continue business as usual. Divide and rule. Unfortunately, it still works.

(34)
They want the masses engaged, with great passion, in activities that are politically meaningless. When that fails, they divide politically minded individuals into groups and set them against each other.

(35)
Racism, religionism, and sexism—what do they all have in common? Each provides an easy path to superior status. Practitioners simply declare that they are, and always will be, inherently superior. That's it. From that point forward, they assume the right to disrespect and abuse their inferiors as much as they want. Pretty clever, huh? Instant, unearned, irrevocable superiority. Fortunately, racism, religionism, and sexism have declined over the past century. *Unfortunately*, the desire for irrevocable superiority has not.

(36)
Strength comes to us through struggle. If we want to experience the next step in human evolution, we'll need to overcome the psychological vulnerabilities that our rulers so easily exploit.

notes:_____

_____

_____

SPIRITUAL

(37)

They come into our lives, they stay as long as they can, and they give us all they've got to give. When it's time for their promotion, we've got to accept it. We've got to be grateful for all that they gave us. If we focus only on wanting more, we ask for something we can never have. It's an error, and we'll suffer dearly for it.

(38)

If your deceased loved one could choose, would they want their memory to be a source of pain for the rest of your life, or would they be a thousand times happier to know that their memory *always* warms your heart and brings a smile to your face?

(39)

Some believe that their suffering proves how much they loved the one that is gone. They cannot see that pinning their misery on the dead isn't a show of love. At best, their perspective erodes gratitude for the tremendous gift they were given. At worst, it provides an excuse to destroy themselves with despair (something their loved one would *never* want them to do).

(40)

Maybe the purpose of life is simple: Learn to overcome the errors that harm us and others.

notes:_____

_____

_____

Index

NOTES

NOTES

NOTES

NOTES

NOTES

NOTES

NOTES

NOTES

NOTES

NOTES

Made in the USA
Columbia, SC
03 December 2023

6a696667-4395-49c8-8647-24a927694f1bR01